Fodor's® Pocket Budapest

SECOND EDITION

D0911987

Excerpted from *Fodor's Eastern and Central Europe*

Fodor's Travel Publications, Inc.
New York • Toronto • London • Sydney • Auckland
www.fodors.com

Fodor's Pocket Budapest

EDITORS: Jennifer J. Paull and Stephanie J. Adler

Editorial Contributors: David Brown, Christina Knight, Matthew Lore, Helayne Schiff, M. T. Schwartzman (Essential Information editor), Julie Tomasz

Editorial Production: Tom Holton

Maps: David Lindroth, *cartographer*; Steven Amsterdam, *map editor*

Design: Fabrizio La Rocca, *creative director*; Guido Caroti, *associate art director*; Lyndell Brookhouse-Gil, *cover designer*; Jolie Novak, *photo editor*

Production/Manufacturing: Mike Costa

Cover Photograph: David Hanson/Tony Stone Images

Copyright

Second edition

ISBN 0–679–00052–6

Special Sales

Fodor's Travel Publications are available at special discounts for bulk purchases for sales promotions or premiums. Special editions, including personalized covers, excerpts of existing guides, and corporate imprints, can be created in large quantities for special needs. For more information, contact your local bookseller or write to Special Markets, Fodor's Travel Publications, 201 East 50th Street, New York, NY 10022. Inquiries from Canada should be directed to your local Canadian bookseller or sent to Random House of Canada, Ltd., Marketing Department, 2775 Matheson Boulevard East, Mississauga, Ontario L4W 4P7. Inquiries from the United Kingdom should be sent to Fodor's Travel Publications, 20 Vauxhall Bridge Road, London SW1V 2SA, England.

PRINTED IN THE UNITED STATES OF AMERICA

10 9 8 7 6 5 4 3 2 1

CONTENTS

Maps

ON THE ROAD WITH FODOR'S

WHEN I PLAN A VA-CATION, the first thing I do is cast around among my friends and colleagues to find someone who's just been where I'm going. That's because there's no substitute for a recommendation from a good friend who knows your tastes, your budget, and your circumstances, someone who's just been there. Unfortunately, such friends are few and far between. So it's nice to know that there's *Fodor's Pocket Budapest*.

In the first place, this book won't stay home when you hit the road. It will accompany you every step of the way, steering you away from wrong turns and wrong choices. Most important of all, it's written and assiduously updated by the kind of people you *would* hit up for travel tips if you knew them. In these pages, they don't send you chasing down every town and sight in Budapest but have instead selected the best ones, the ones that are worthy of your time and money. Will this be the vacation of your dreams? We hope so.

About Our Writer

Julie Tomasz, a travel and fiction writer of Hungarian descent, updated all of the material in this book. She lived in Budapest for three years working as a founding editor of the *Budapest Sun,* and has been writing and editing for Fodor's for nine years. Hopelessly in love with Budapest and having acquired Hungarian citizenship, Julie plans to divide her time between the United States and Hungary.

We would also like to thank the national and local tourist offices of Hungary and Budapest for their help with questions great and small.

We gratefully acknowledge Malév Hungarian Airlines for its help with realizing this book.

Connections

We're pleased that the American Society of Travel Agents continues to endorse Fodor's as its guidebook of choice. ASTA is the world's largest and most influential travel trade association, operating in more than 170 countries, with 27,000 members pledged to adhere to a strict code of ethics reflecting the Society's motto, "Integrity in Travel." ASTA shares Fodor's devotion to providing smart, honest travel information and advice to travelers, and we've long recommended that our readers—even those who have guidebooks and traveling friends—consult ASTA member agents for the experience and professionalism they bring to your vacation planning.

On Fodor's Web site (www.fodors.com), check out the Resource Center, an on-line companion to the Essential Information section of this book, complete with useful hot links to related sites. In our forums, you can also get lively advice from other travelers and more great tips from Fodor's experts worldwide.

How to Use This Book

Organization

Up front is **Essential Information,** an easy-to-use section arranged alphabetically by topic. Under each listing you'll find tips and information that will help you accomplish what you need to in Budapest.

The first chapter in the guide, **Destination: Budapest,** helps get you in the mood for your trip. Pleasures and Pastimes describes the activities and sights that make Budapest unique, and Quick Tours lays out a selection of half-day itineraries that will help you make the most of your time in Budapest.

The **Exploring Budapest** chapter is divided into nine neighborhoods. Each lists sights alphabetically and has a suggested walk that will take you around to the major sights.

The remaining chapters are arranged in alphabetical order by subject—**Dining, Lodging, Nightlife and the Arts, Shopping,** and **Side Trip: The Danube Bend.**

Icons and Symbols

★ Our special recommendations
✕ Restaurant
🏨 Lodging establishment
🐤 Good for kids (rubber duck)
☞ Sends you to another section of the guide for more information
✉ Address
☎ Telephone number
🕓 Opening and closing times
💷 Admission prices (those we give apply to adults; substantially reduced fees are almost always available for children, students, and senior citizens)

Numbers in white and black circles (e.g., ③ ❸) that appear on the maps, in the margins, and within the tours correspond to one another.

Dining and Lodging

The restaurants and lodgings we list are the cream of the crop in each price range. Price charts appear in the introductions to Chapter 3 and Chapter 4.

Hotel Facilities

We always list the facilities that are available—but we don't specify whether you'll be charged extra to use them: When pricing accommodations, always ask what's included. In addition, assume that all rooms have private baths unless noted otherwise. In addition, when you book a room, be sure to mention if you have a disability or are traveling with children, if you prefer a private bath or a certain type of bed, or if you have specific dietary needs or other concerns.

Assume that hotels operate on the **European Plan** (EP, with no meals) unless we specify that they include breakfast or other meals in the rates.

Restaurant Reservations and Dress Codes

Reservations are always a good idea; we mention them only when they're essential or are not accepted. Book as far ahead as you can, and reconfirm as soon as you arrive. Unless otherwise noted, the restaurants listed are open daily for lunch and dinner. We mention dress only when men are required to wear a jacket or a jacket and tie. Look for an overview of local dining-out habits in the Pleasures and Pastimes section of Chapter 1 and in Chapter 3.

Credit Cards

The following abbreviations are used: **AE**, American Express; **DC**, Diners Club; **MC**, MasterCard; and **V**, Visa.

Don't Forget to Write

You can use this book in the confidence that all prices and opening times are based on information supplied to us at press time; Fodor's cannot accept responsibility for any errors. Time inevitably brings changes, so always confirm information when it matters—especially if you're making a detour to visit a specific place.

Were the restaurants we recommended as described? Did our hotel picks exceed your expectations? Did you find a museum we recommended a waste of time? Keeping a travel guide fresh and up-to-date is a big job, and we welcome your feedback, positive *and* negative. If you have complaints, we'll look into them and revise our entries when the facts warrant it. If you've discovered a special place that we haven't included, we'll pass the information along to our correspondents and have them check it out. So send us your thoughts via e-mail at editors@fodors.com (specifying the name of the book on the subject line) or on paper in care of the Budapest editor at Fodor's, 201 East 50th Street, New York, New York 10022. In the meantime, have a wonderful trip!

Karen Cure

Karen Cure
Editorial Director

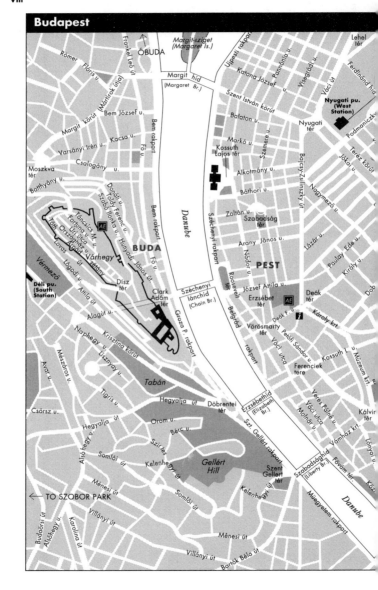

Budapest

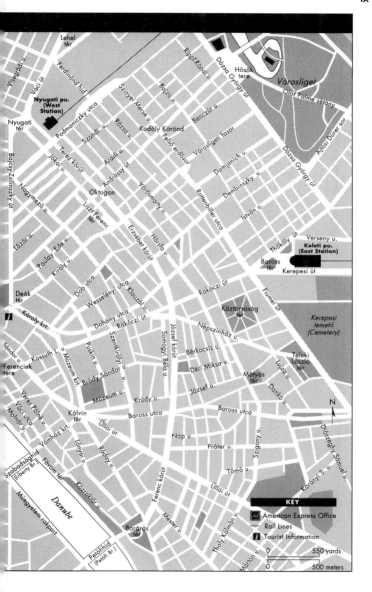

Lehel tér
Ferdinánd híd
Vágradi u.
Vác út
Dózsa György út
Ript Rónai u.
Hősök tere
Városliget
Olof Palme sétány
Nyugati pu. (West Station)
Szinyei Merse u.
Bajza u.
Benczúr u.
Aitosi Dürer sor
Dózsa György út
Nyugati tér
Podmaniczky utca
Rózsa u.
Kodály Körönd
Felső erdősor
Városligeti fasor
Szondi u.
Terèz körút
Aradi u.
Andrássy út
Damjanich u.
Bajcsy-Zsilinszky út
Jókai u.
Nagymező u.
Oktogon
Vörösmarty u.
Dembinszky u.
István u.
Lázár u.
Liszt Ferenc tér
Erzsébet körút
Paulay Ede u.
Hársfa u.
Thököly út
Verseny u.
Keleti pu. (East Station)
Király u.
Baross tér
Kerepesi út
Deák tér
Dob utca
Wesselényi utca
Klauzál u.
Rákóczi út
Fiumei út
Kerepesi temető (Cemetery)
Károly krt.
Dohány utca
Rákóczi út
Köztársaság tér
Sándor u.
Kossuth L. u.
Szentkirályi u.
József körút
Somogyi Béla u.
Népszinház u.
Bérkocsis u.
Teleki László tér
Ferenciek tere
Puskin u.
Múzeum krt.
Bródy Sándor u.
Déri Miksa u.
Luzsa u.
Dankó u.
Veres Pálne u.
Múzeum u.
Krúdy u.
Mátyás tér
József u.
Vaci utca
Kálvin tér
Baross utca
Baross utca
Molnár u.
Üllői út
Nap u.
Szigony u.
Vámház krt.
Ványai u.
Práter u.
Diószeghy Sámuel u.
Szabadsághíd (Liberty Br.)
Fővám tér
Ráday u.
Tömő u.
Korányi S. u.
Köztakár u.
Üllői út
Danube
Ferenc körút
Thaly Kálmán u.
Műegyetem rakpart
Mester u.
KEY
Boráros tér
Márton u.
Petőfihíd (Petőfi Br.)

KEY

Ae American Express Office
— Rail Lines
i Tourist Information

N

0   550 yards
0   500 meters

Magyarország (Hungary)

AKIA
Aggtelek Sárospatak   Sátoraljaújhely   UKRAINE
Kazinbarcika   Kisvárda
Ózd   Tokaj   Vásárosnamény
22   Mátészalka
algótarján   Eger   Leninváros   Miskolc   41
Gyöngyös   Mezőkövesd   Nyíregyháza   Nyírbátor
atvan   Hajdúböszörmény
         Heves   Tiszafüred   Debrecen
öllő   Kiskőrei   Hortobágy
         Jászberény   Reservoir
est   Karcag   Hajdúszoboszló
E60   Kisujszállás
Cegléd   Törökszentmiklós
         Szolnok   Túrkeve
gykörös   Kecskemét   Szarvas
egyháza   Csongrád   Békés
körös   Békéscsaba   ROMANIA
         Szentes   Orosháza   Gyula
53   Kőrös River
Kiskunhalas   Hódmezővásárhely
         Szeged   N
55   Makó
E68   0   100 miles
E75
TO   0   150 km
GRADE   SERBIA

ESSENTIAL INFORMATION

Basic Information on Traveling in Budapest,
Savvy Tips to Make Your Trip a Breeze, and
Companies and Organizations to Contact

AIR TRAVEL

Ferihegy, Hungary's only commercial airport, is about 22 km (14 mi) southeast of Budapest. All Malév flights operate from the newer Terminal 2, 4 km (2½ mi) farther from the city; other airlines use Terminal 1.

Flying time is 2½ hours from London, 16 hours from Los Angeles, 7½ hours from Montreal, and 9 hours from New York.

➤ AIRPORT INFORMATION: **Budapest Ferihegy Repülőtér** (Budapest Ferihegy Airport; ☎ 1/296–9696, 1/296–7155 for same-day flight information).

CARRIERS

The most convenient way to fly between Hungary and the United States is with **Malév Hungarian Airlines** nonstop direct service between JFK International Airport in New York and Budapest's Ferihegy Airport—the only nonstop flight that exists. The service runs daily most of the year. **British Airways** and Malév offer daily nonstop service between Budapest and London.

➤ MAJOR AIRLINES: **Continental** (☎ 800/231–0856). **Delta** (☎ 800/241–4141). **Northwest** (☎ 800/447–4747). **United** (☎ 800/538–2929).

➤ REGIONAL CARRIERS: **Malév Hungarian Airlines** (in Budapest, ☎ 1/235–3535 or 06/80–212–121 toll free; 1/235–3804 [ticketing]) has regular nonstop flights between the United States and Budapest.

➤ FROM THE U.K.: **British Airways** (✉ 156 Regent St., London W1R 5TA, ☎ 0181/897–4000; outside London, 0345/222–111).

TRANSFERS

Many hotels offer their guests car or minibus transportation to and from Ferihegy, but all of them charge for the service. You should arrange for a pickup in advance. If you're taking a taxi, allow 40 minutes during nonpeak hours and at least an hour during rush hours (7 AM–9 AM from the airport, 4 PM–6 PM from the city). Official Airport Taxis are queued at the exit and overseen by a taxi monitor; rates are fixed according to the zone of your final destination. A taxi ride to the center of Budapest will cost around 3,500 Ft. There's also a special 1,990-Ft. rate to the airport if you call one day in advance to arrange for a pickup. Avoid taxi drivers who approach before you are out of the arrivals lounge.

LRI Centrum-Airport-Centrum minibuses run every half hour from 5:30 AM to 9:30 PM to and from the Erzsébet tér bus station (Platform 1) in downtown Budapest. It takes almost the same time as taxis but costs only 700 Ft. The LRI Airport Shuttle provides convenient door-to-door service between the airport and any address in the city. To get to the airport, call to arrange a pickup; to get to the city, make arrangements at LRI's airport desk. Service to or from either terminal costs around 1,400 Ft. per person; since it normally shuttles several people at once, remember to allow time for a few other pickups or dropoffs.

➤ TAXIS & SHUTTLES: **Airport Taxis** (☎ 1/282–2222). **LRI Airport Shuttle** (☎ 1/296–8555 or 1/296–6283). **LRI Centrum-Airport-Centrum** (☎ 1/296–8555 or 1/296–6283).

BUS TRAVEL

For information on bus travel within Budapest, *see* Public Transportation, *below.*

BUSINESS HOURS

Banks are generally open weekdays 8–2 or 3, often with a one-hour lunch break at around noon; most close at 1 on Fridays. Museums are generally open Tuesday through Sunday from 10 to 6 and are closed on Mondays; most stop admitting people 30 minutes before closing time. Department stores are open weekdays 10–5 or 6, Saturdays until 1. Grocery stores are generally open weekdays from 7 AM to 6 or 7 PM, Saturdays until 1 PM; "nonstops," or *éjjeli-nappali,* are (theoretically) open 24 hours.

CAR RENTAL

All the major car-rental agencies have outlets in Budapest, but rates are high: Daily rates for automatics begin around $55–$60 plus 60¢ per km (½ mi); personal, theft, and accident insurance (not required but recommended) runs an additional $25–$30 per day. Rates tend to be significantly lower if you arrange your rental *from home* through the American offices. Smaller local companies, on the other hand, can rent Hungarian cars for as little as $150 per week.

Foreign driver's licenses are generally acceptable by car rental agencies but are technically not valid legally; they are almost always accepted by the police, but it can get messy and expensive if you are stopped by a police officer who insists you need an International Driver's License (which, legally, you do).

➤ MAJOR AGENCIES: **Avis** (☎ 800/331–1084; 800/879–2847 in Canada). **Budget** (☎ 800/527–0700; 0800/181181 in the U.K.).

Dollar (☎ 800/800–4000; 0990/ 565656 in the U.K., where it is known as Eurodollar). **Hertz** (☎ 800/654–3001; 800/263–0600 in Canada; 0345/555888 in the U.K.).

The Budapest offices for these agencies are: **Avis** (main office, ✉ V, Szervita tér 8, ☎ 1/318–4240; Terminal 1, ☎ 1/296–6421; Terminal 2, ☎ 1/296–7265). **Budget-Pannonia** (main office, ✉ Hotel Mercure Buda, I, Krisztina körút 41–43, ☎ 1/356–6333; Terminal 1, ☎ 1/296–8197; Terminal 2, ☎ 1/296–8481). **Hertz** (also known in Hungary as Mercure Rent-a-Car; ✉ V, Marriott Hotel, Apáczai Csere János u. 4, ☎ 1/266–4361; Terminal 1, ☎ 1/296–7171; Terminal 2, ☎ 1/296–6988).

➤ LOCAL AGENCIES: **Americana Rent-a-Car** (✉ Ibis Hotel Volga, XIII, Dózsa György út 65, ☎ 1/ 270–2542; 1/320–8287). **Fötaxi** (main office, ✉ VII, Kertész u. 24–28, ☎ 1/322–1471; Terminal 1, ☎ 1/296–8629; Terminal 2, ☎ 1/296–8606).

CAR TRAVEL

Budapest, like any Western city, is plagued by traffic jams during the day, but motorists should have no problem later in the evening. Motorists not accustomed to sharing the city streets with trams should pay extra attention. You should be prepared to be flagged down numerous times by police conducting routine checks for drunk driving and stolen cars. Be sure all of your papers are in order and readily accessible; unfortunately, the police have been known to give foreigners a hard time.

A word of caution: If you have any alcohol whatsoever in your body, do not drive. Penalties are fierce, and the blood-alcohol limit in Hungary is *zero*.

AUTO CLUBS

➤ IN HUNGARY: **Hungarian Automobile Club** (✉ Budapest XIV, Francia út 38/B, ☎ 088).

➤ IN CANADA: **Canadian Automobile Association** (CAA, ☎ 613/ 247–0117).

➤ IN THE U.K.: **Automobile Association** (AA, ☎ 0990/500–600), **Royal Automobile Club** (RAC, ☎ 0990/722–722 for membership, 0345/121–345 for insurance).

➤ IN THE U.S.: **American Automobile Association** (AAA, ☎ 800/ 564–6222).

PARKING

Gone are the "anything goes" days of parking in Budapest, when cars parked for free practically anywhere in the city, straddling curbs or angled in the middle of sidewalks. Now most streets in Budapest's main districts have restricted, fee parking; there are either parking meters that accept coins or attendants who approach your car as you park and charge you according to how many hours you intend to stay. Hourly rates average 140 Ft.

In most cases, overnight parking in these areas is free. Budapest also has a number of parking lots and a few garages; two central-Pest locations are: V, Szervita tér and V, Aranykéz u. 4–6.

ROADS

The main routes into Budapest are the M1 from Vienna (via Győr), the M3 from near Gyöngyös, the M5 from Kecskemét, and the M7 from the Balaton; the M3 and M5 are being upgraded over the next few years and extended to Hungary's borders with Slovakia and Serbia.

CUSTOMS & DUTIES

ON ARRIVAL IN HUNGARY

If you are over 16, you may bring in 500 cigarettes or 100 cigars or 500 grams of tobacco, plus 1 liter of wine, 1 liter of spirits, 5 liters of beer, and 0.25 liters of perfume. A customs charge is made on gifts valued in Hungary at more than 21,000 Ft.

ON DEPARTURE FROM HUNGARY

Take care when you leave Hungary that you have the right documentation for exporting goods. Keep receipts of any items bought from Konsumtourist, Intertourist, or Képcsarnok Vállalat. A special permit is needed for works of art, antiques, or objects of museum value. Upon leaving, you are entitled to a value-added tax (VAT) refund on new goods (i.e., not works of art, antiques, or objects of museum value) valued at more than 25,000 Ft. (VAT inclusive). But applying for the refund may rack up more frustration than money: Cash refunds are given only in forints, and you may find yourself in the airport minutes before boarding with a handful of soft currency, of which no more than 10,000 Ft. may be taken out of the country. If you made your purchases by credit card you can file for a credit to your card or to your bank account (again in forints), but don't expect it to come through in a hurry. If you intend to apply for the credit, make sure you get customs to stamp the original purchase invoice before you leave the country.

➤ INFORMATION: For more information, pick up a tax refund brochure from any tourist office or hotel, or contact **Intel Trade Rt.** (✉ I, Csalogány u. 6–10, ☏ 1/201–8120 or 1/356–9800). For further Hungarian customs information, inquire at the **National Customs and Revenue Office** (✉ IX, Mester u. 7, Budapest, ☏ 1/218–0017).

IN CANADA

Canadian residents who have been out of Canada for at least 7 days may bring in C$500 worth of goods duty-free. If you meet the age requirements of the province or territory through which you reenter Canada, you may bring in, duty-free, 1.14 liters (40 imperial ounces) of wine or liquor *or* 24

12-ounce cans or bottles of beer or ale. If you are 16 or older you may bring in, duty-free, 200 cigarettes and 50 cigars. You may send an unlimited number of gifts worth up to C$60 each duty-free to Canada. Label the package UNSOLICITED GIFT—VALUE UNDER $60. Alcohol and tobacco are excluded.

➤ INFORMATION: **Revenue Canada** (✉ 2265 St. Laurent Blvd. S, Ottawa, Ontario K1G 4K3, ☎ 613/993–0534, 800/461–9999 in Canada).

IN THE U.K.
You may import, duty-free, 200 cigarettes or 50 cigars; 1 liter of spirits or 2 liters of fortified or sparkling wine or liqueurs; 2 liters of still table wine; 60 milliliters of perfume; 250 milliliters of toilet water; plus £136 worth of other goods, including gifts and souvenirs.

➤ INFORMATION: **HM Customs and Excise** (✉ Dorset House, Stamford St., London SE1 9NG, ☎ 0171/202–4227).

IN THE U.S.
U.S. residents may bring home $400 worth of foreign goods duty-free if they've been out of the country for at least 48 hours. U.S. residents 21 and older may bring back 1 liter of alcohol duty-free. In addition, regardless of your age, you are allowed 200 cigarettes and 100 non-Cuban cigars. Antiques, which the U.S. Customs Service defines as objects more than 100 years old, enter duty-free, as do original works of art done entirely by hand, including paintings, drawings, and sculptures. You may also send packages home duty-free: up to $200 worth of goods for personal use, with a limit of one parcel per addressee per day; label the package PERSONAL USE, and attach a list of its contents and their retail value.

➤ INFORMATION: **U.S. Customs Service** (Inquiries, ✉ Box 7407, Washington, DC 20044, ☎ 202/927–6724).

DINING

See Pleasures and Pastimes *in* Chapter 1, *and* Chapter 3.

DISABILITIES & ACCESSIBILITY

ACCESS IN EASTERN AND CENTRAL EUROPE

Provisions for travelers with disabilities in Budapest are extremely limited; probably the best solution is to travel with a nondisabled companion. While many hotels, especially large American or international chains, offer some wheelchair-accessible rooms, special facilities at museums, restaurants, and on public transportation are difficult to find.

➤ LOCAL RESOURCES: Contact the **Mozgáskorlátozottak Egyesületeinek Országos Szövetsége** (National Association of People with Mobility Impairments, or MEOSZ; ✉ 1032 Budapest, San

Marco u. 76, ☎ 1/388–8951) for information on special services and accommodations.

DISCOUNTS & DEALS

CREDIT-CARD BENEFITS

When you use your credit card to make travel purchases you may get free travel-accident insurance, collision-damage insurance, and medical or legal assistance, depending on the card and the bank that issued it. American Express, MasterCard, and Visa provide one or more of these services, so **get a copy of your credit card's travel-benefits policy.**

DISCOUNT RESERVATIONS

➤ AIRLINE TICKETS: ☎ 800/FLY–4–LESS.

➤ HOTEL ROOMS: **Hotels Plus** (☎ 800/235–0909). **International Marketing & Travel Concepts** (☎ 800/790–4682). **Steigenberger Reservation Service** (☎ 800/223–5652). **Travel Interlink** (☎ 800/888–5898).

SENIOR-CITIZEN DISCOUNTS

To qualify for age-related discounts, **mention your senior-citizen status up front** when booking hotel reservations (not when checking out) and before you're seated in restaurants (not when paying the bill). Note that discounts may be limited to certain menus, days, or hours. When renting a car, **ask about promotional car-rental discounts,** which can be cheaper than senior-citizen rates.

➤ LOCAL DISCOUNTS: In Hungary, non-Hungarian senior citizens (men over 60, women over 55) are eligible for a 20% discount on rail travel. Contact or visit **MÁV Passenger Service** (✉ Andrassy út 35, Budapest VI, ☎ 1/322–8275) for information.

STUDENT DISCOUNTS

In Hungary, as a general rule, only Hungarian citizens and students at Hungarian institutions qualify for student discounts on domestic travel fares and admission fees. Travelers under 25, however, qualify for excellent youth rates on international airfares; those under 26 are eligible for youth rates on international train fares. The International Student Identity Card (ISIC) is accepted in Budapest and other large Hungarian cities, but not as widely as it is in Western countries.

ELECTRICITY

To use your U.S.-purchased electric-powered equipment, **bring a converter and adapter.** The electrical current in Hungary is 220 volts, 50 cycles alternating current (AC); wall outlets generally take plugs with two round prongs.

EMERGENCIES

Emergency contact numbers in Budapest are: **Ambulance** (☎ 104); **Fire** (☎ 105); **Hungarian Automobile Club**'s Yellow Angels breakdown service (☎ 088); **Police** (☎ 107). For medical emergency contacts, *see also* Health, *below.*

LATE-NIGHT PHARMACIES
The state-run pharmacies close between 6 and 8 PM, but several pharmacies stay open at night and on the weekend, offering 24-hour service, with a small surcharge for items that aren't officially stamped as urgent by a physician. You must ring the buzzer next to the night window and someone will respond over the intercom. Staff is unlikely to speak English. Central ones in Pest include those at **Teréz körút 41** (☎ 1/311–4439) in the sixth district, near the Nyugati Train Station; and the one at **Rákóczi út 39** (☎ 1/314–3695) in the 8th district, near the Keleti Train Station. In Buda, there is one across the street from the Déli train station at **Alkotás utca 1/b** (☎ 1/355–4691), in the 12th district.

ENGLISH-LANGUAGE PERIODICALS

Several English-language weekly newspapers have sprouted up to placate Budapest's large expatriate community. The *Budapest Sun, Budapest Week,* and the *Budapest Business Journal* are sold at major newsstands, hotels, and tourist points.

HEALTH

You may gain weight, but there are few other serious health hazards for the traveler in Budapest. Tap water tastes bad but is generally drinkable; when it runs rusty out of the tap or the aroma of chlorine is overpowering, it might help to have some iodine tablets or bottled water handy. Vegetarians and those on special diets may have a problem with the heavy local cuisine, which is based almost exclusively on pork and beef.

➤ EMERGENCY CONTACTS: **Ambulance** (☎ 104), or call **Falck–SOS** (✉ II, Kapy u. 49/b, ☎ 1/200–0100 or 1/200–0122), a 24-hour private ambulance service with English-speaking personnel. **Doctor:** Ask your hotel or embassy for recommendations or visit the **R-Clinic** (✉ II, Felsőzöldmáli út 13, ☎ 1/325–9999), a private clinic staffed by English-speaking doctors offering 24-hour medical and ambulance service. **Dentist: Professional Dental Associates** (✉ II, Sobrás u. 9, ☎ 1/200–4447 or 1/200–4448) is a private, English-speaking dental practice consisting of Western-trained dentists and hygienists; service is available 24 hours a day. **Police** (☎ 107).

HOLIDAYS

January 1; March 15 (Anniversary of 1848 Revolution); April 4–5, 1999, April 22–23, 2000 (Easter and Easter Monday); May 1 (Labor Day); May 23–24, 1999 (Pentecost); August 20 (St. Stephen's and Constitution Day); October 23 (1956 Revolution Day); December 24–26.

LANGUAGE

Hungarian (*Magyar*) tends to look and sound intimidating at first because it is not an Indo-European language. Generally, older people speak some German, and many younger people speak at least rudimentary English, which has become the most popular language to learn. It's a safe bet that anyone in the tourist trade will speak at least one of the two languages.

LODGING

See Pleasures and Pastimes *in* Chapter 1, *and* Chapter 4.

MAIL

Airmail letters and postcards generally take seven days to travel between Hungary and the United States, sometimes more than twice as long, however, during the Christmas season.

Postage for an airmail letter to the United States costs about 125 Ft.; an airmail letter to the United Kingdom and elsewhere in Western Europe costs about 115 Ft. Airmail postcards to the United States cost about 85 Ft. and to the United Kingdom and the rest of Western Europe, about 80 Ft.

MONEY

Hungary's unit of currency is the forint (Ft.). There are bills of 50, 100, 200, 500, 1,000, 2,000, 5,000, and 10,000 forints; and coins of 1, 2, 5, 10, 20, 50, 100, and 200 forints. The exchange rate was approximately 205 Ft. to the U.S. dollar, 142 Ft. to the Canadian dollar, and 338 Ft. to

the pound sterling at press time. Although cash card and Eurocheque facilities are becoming easier to find in big cities, it is probably still wise to bring traveler's checks, which can be cashed all over the country in banks and hotels.

CREDIT & DEBIT CARDS

Both credit and debit cards will get you cash advances at ATMs worldwide if your card is properly programmed with your personal identification number (PIN). For use in Hungary, your PIN must be four digits long.

➤ ATM LOCATIONS: **Cirrus** (☎ 800/424–7787). **Plus** (☎ 800/843–7587) for locations in the U.S. and Canada, or visit your local bank.

EXCHANGING MONEY

You should **change money at banks** for the most favorable exchange rate. Although fees charged for ATM transactions may be higher abroad than at home, Cirrus and Plus exchange rates are excellent, because they are based on wholesale rates offered only by major banks. You often won't do as well at exchange booths in airports or rail and bus stations, in hotels, in restaurants, or in stores, although you may find their hours more convenient. To avoid lines at airport exchange booths, **get a bit of local currency before you leave home.**

SAMPLE COSTS

Cup of coffee, 100 Ft.; bottle of beer, 300 Ft.–400 Ft.; soft drinks, 100 Ft.; ham sandwich, 150 Ft.; 2-km (1-mi) taxi ride, 150 Ft.; museum admission, 100 Ft.–250 Ft.

PASSPORTS & VISAS

When traveling internationally, **carry a passport even if you don't need one** (it's always the best form of I.D.), and make **two photocopies of the data page** (one for someone at home and another for you, carried separately from your passport). If you lose your passport, promptly call the nearest embassy or consulate and the local police.

Canadian, U.K., and U.S. citizens need a valid passport to enter Hungary for stays of up to 90 days.

PASSPORT OFFICES

➤ CANADIAN CITIZENS: **Passport Office** (☎ 819/994–3500 or 800/567–6868).

➤ U.K. CITIZENS: **London Passport Office** (☎ 0990/21010), for fees and documentation requirements and to request an emergency passport.

➤ U.S. CITIZENS: **National Passport Information Center** (☎ 900/225–5674; calls are charged at 35¢ per minute for automated service, $1.05 per minute for operator service).

PUBLIC TRANSPORTATION

BY BUS AND TRAM

Trams (*villamos*) and buses (*autóbusz*) are abundant and convenient. One fare ticket (80 Ft.; valid on all forms of public transportation) is valid for only one ride in one direction. Tickets cannot be bought on board; they are widely available in metro stations and newsstands and must be canceled on board—watch how other passengers do it—unless you've purchased a *napijegy* (day ticket, 600 Ft.; a three-day "tourist ticket" costs 1,200 Ft.), which allows unlimited travel on all services within the city limits. Hold on to whatever ticket you have; spot-checks by aggressive undercover checkers (look for the red armbands) are numerous and often targeted at tourists. Trolley-bus stops are marked with red, rectangular signs that list the route stops; regular bus stops are marked with similar light blue signs. (The trolley-buses and regular buses themselves are red and blue, respectively.) Tram stops are marked by light blue or yellow signs. Most lines run from 5 AM and stop operating at 11 PM, but there is all-night service on certain key lines. Consult the separate night-bus map posted in most metro stations for all-night routes.

BY SUBWAY

Service on Budapest's subways is cheap, fast, frequent, and comfortable; stations are easily located on maps and streets by the big letter M (for metro). Tickets—80 Ft.; valid on all forms of mass transportation—can be bought at hotels, metro stations, newsstands, and kiosks. They are valid for one ride only; you can't change lines or direction. Tickets must be canceled in the time-clock machines in station entrances and should be kept until the end of the journey, as there are frequent checks by undercover inspectors; a fine for traveling without a validated ticket is about 1,000 Ft. A *napijegy* (day ticket) costs 600 Ft. (a three-day "tourist ticket," 1,200 Ft.) and allows unlimited travel on all services within the city limits.

Line 1 (marked FÖLDALATTI), which starts downtown at Vörösmarty tér and follows Andrássy út out past Gundel restaurant and City Park, is an antique tourist attraction in itself, built in the 1890s for the Magyar Millennium; its yellow trains with tank treads still work. Lines 2 and 3 were built 90 years later. Line 2 (red) runs from the eastern suburbs, past the Keleti (Eastern) Station, through the Inner City area, and under the Danube to the Déli (Southern) Station. (One of the stations, Moszkva tér, is where the *Várbusz* [Castle Bus] can be boarded.) Line 3 (blue) runs from the southern suburbs to Deák tér, through the Inner City, and northward to the Nyugati (West) Station and the northern suburbs. On all three lines, fare tickets are canceled in machines at the station entrance. All three metro lines meet at the Deák tér station and run from 4:30 AM to shortly after 11 PM.

SAFETY

Crime rates are relatively low in Hungary, but travelers should beware of pickpockets in crowded areas, especially on public transportation, at railway stations, and in big hotels. In general, always keep your valuables with you—in open bars and restaurants, purses hung on or placed next to chairs are easy targets. Make sure your wallet is safe in a buttoned pocket, or watch your handbag.

SIGHTSEEING TOURS

BOAT TOURS

From late March through October boats leave from the dock at Vigadó tér on 1½-hour cruises between the railroad bridges north and south of the Árpád and Petőfi bridges, respectively. The trip, organized by MAHART Tours, runs only on weekends and holidays (once a day, at noon) from March until May, then twice daily from May to October (at noon and 7 PM); the cost is about 800 Ft. From mid-June through August, the evening cruise leaves at 7:45 PM and features live music and dancing for 100 Ft. more.

The *Duna-Bella* takes guests on two-hour tours on the Danube, including a one-hour walk on Margaret Island and shipboard cocktails. Recorded commentary is provided through earphones. The tour is offered July through August, six times a day; September, three times a day; and October and November, once a day. Boats depart from Pier 6–7 at Vigadó tér.

➤ TOUR COMPANIES: *Duna-Bella* (☎ 1/317–2203 for reservations and information). **MAHART Tours** (☎ 1/318–1704).

BUS TOURS

IBUSZ Travel conducts three-hour orientation tours of the city that operate all year and cost about 4,000 Ft. Starting from Erzsébet tér, they take in parts of both Buda and Pest. Gray Line Cityrama also offers a three-hour city bus tour (about 4,000 Ft. per person). Both have commentary in English.

➤ TOUR COMPANIES: **Gray Line Cityrama** (✉ V, Báthori u. 22, ☎ 1/302–4382). **IBUSZ Travel** (✉ Rubin Aktiv Hotel, XI, Dajka Gábor u. 3, ☎ 1/319–7520, 1/319–7519).

TAXIS

Taxis are plentiful and a good value, but make sure they have a working meter. The average initial charge is 50 Ft.–75 Ft., plus about 110 Ft. per km (½ mi) and 30 Ft. per minute of waiting time. Many drivers try to charge outrageous prices, especially if they sense that their passenger is a tourist. Avoid

unmarked "freelance" taxis; stick with those affiliated with an established company. Your safest and most reliable bet is to do what the locals do: Order a taxi by phone; it will arrive in about five to 10 minutes.

➤ TAXI COMPANIES: **Citytaxi** (☎ 1/211–1111). **Fő taxi** (☎ 1/222–2222).

TELEPHONES

The country code for Hungary is 36. When dialing from outside the country, drop the initial zero from the area code. The city code for Budapest is 1; it is unnecessary to use this code when calling within the city. Dial 198 for directory assistance for all of Hungary.

INTERNATIONAL CALLS

Direct calls to foreign countries can be made from Budapest and all major provincial towns by dialing 00 and waiting for the international dialing tone; on pay phones the initial charge is 60 Ft.

➤ TO OBTAIN ACCESS CODES: **AT&T** (☎ 00–800–01111). **MCI** (☎ 00–800–01411). **Sprint** (☎ 00–800–01877).

PAY PHONES

Coin-operated pay phones use 20 Ft. coins—the cost of a three-minute local call—and also accept 10-Ft. and 50-Ft. coins. Gray card-operated telephones outnumber coin-operated phones in Budapest. The cards—available at post offices and most newsstands and kiosks—come in units of 50 (800 Ft.) and 120 (1,800 Ft.) calls.

TIPPING

Four decades of socialism have not restrained the extended palm in Hungary—so tip when in doubt. Taxi drivers expect 10% to 15% tips, while porters should get a dollar or two. Coatroom attendants receive 100 to 200 Ft., as do gas-pump attendants if they wash your windows or check your tires. Gratuities are not included automatically to restaurant bills; when the waiter arrives with the bill, you should immediately add a 10% to 15% tip to the amount, as it is not customary to leave the tip on the table. If a Gypsy band plays exclusively for your table, you can leave 200 Ft. in a plate discreetly provided for that purpose.

TRAIN TRAVEL

The Hungarian Railroad Inter-City express—which links the country's major cities—is comfortable, clean, fast, and almost always on time; a *helyjegy* (seat reservation), which costs about 300 Ft., is advisable. Remember to take *gyorsvonat* (express trains) and not *személyvonat* (locals), which are extremely slow. On timetables, tracks (*vágány*) are abbreviated with a "v"; *indul* means departing, while *érkezik* means arriving.

➤ RAIL INFORMATION: **MAV Passenger Service** (⊠ Andrassy út 35, Budapest VI, ☎ 1/322–8275, 1/ 342–9150 international information, 1/322–7860 domestic information).

VISITOR INFORMATION

➤ VISITOR INFORMATION: **Budapest Tourist** (⊠ V, Roosevelt tér 5, ☎ 1/317–3555). **IBUSZ** (central branch: ⊠ V, Ferenciek tere 10, ☎ 1/318–6866). **IBUSZ Welcome Hotel Service** (⊠ Apáczai Csere János u. 1, ☎ 1/318–3925 or 1/ 318–5776, FAX 1/317–9099), open 24 hours. **Tourinform** (⊠ V, Sütő u. 2, ☎ 1/317–9800). **Tourism Office of Budapest** (⊠ V, Március 15 tér 7, ☎ 1/266–0479; ⊠ VI, Nyugati pályaudvar, ☎ 1/302– 8580). The **Tourism Office of Budapest** (☞ *above*) has developed the **Budapest Card,** which entitles holders to unlimited travel on public transportation; free admission to many museums and sights; and discounts on various services from participating businesses. The cost (at press time) is 2,000 Ft. for two days, 2,500 Ft. for three days; one card is valid for an adult plus one child under 14.

WHEN TO GO

Budapest is beautiful year-round, but avoid midsummer (especially July and August) and the Christmas and Easter holidays, when it is choked with visitors.

CLIMATE

The following are the average daily maximum and minimum temperatures for Budapest.

Jan.	34F	1C	May	72F	22C	Sept.	73F	23C
	25	− 4		52	11		54	12
Feb.	39F	4C	June	79F	26C	Oct.	61F	16C
	28	− 2		59	15		45	7
Mar.	50F	10C	July	82F	28C	Nov.	46F	8C
	36	2		61	16		37	3
Apr.	63F	17C	Aug.	81F	27C	Dec.	39F	4C
	25	− 4		61	16		30	− 1

1 Destination: Budapest

MAJESTY ON THE DANUBE

SITUATED ON BOTH
BANKS of the Danube,
Budapest unites the col-
orful hills of Buda and the wide,
businesslike boulevards of Pest.
Though it was the site of a Roman
outpost during the 1st century,
the city was not officially created
until 1873, when the towns of
Óbuda, Pest, and Buda were
joined. Since then, Budapest has
been the cultural, political, intel-
lectual, and commercial heart of
Hungary; for the 20% of the nation's population who live in the
capital, anywhere else is simply
vidék ("the country").

Budapest has suffered many rav-
ages in the course of its long history. It was totally destroyed by
the Mongols in 1241, captured by
the Turks in 1541, and nearly destroyed again by Soviet troops in
1945. But this bustling industrial
and cultural center survived as
the capital of the People's Republic of Hungary after the war—
and then, as the 1980s drew to a
close, it became one of the Eastern Bloc's few thriving bastions
of capitalism. Today, judging by
the city's flourishing cafés and
restaurants, markets and bars,
the stagnation enforced by the
Communists seems a thing of the
very distant past.

Much of the charm of a visit to Budapest lies in unexpected glimpses
into shadowy courtyards and in
long vistas down sunlit cobbled
streets. Although some 30,000
buildings were destroyed during
World War II and in 1956, the
past lingers on in the often crumbling architectural details of the
antique structures that remain.

Pleasures and Pastimes

Dining

Through the lean postwar years
the Hungarian kitchen lost none
of its spice and sparkle. Meats,
rich sauces, and creamy desserts
predominate, but the more health-
conscious will also find salads,
even out of season. (Strict vegetarians should note, however, that
even meatless dishes are usually
cooked with lard [*zsír*].) In addition to the ubiquitous dishes with
which most foreigners are famil-
iar, such as chunky beef *gulyás*
(goulash) and *paprikás csirke*
(chicken paprika) served with
galuska (little pinched dumplings),
traditional Hungarian classics include fiery *halászlé* (fish soup),
scarlet with hot paprika; *fogas*
(pike perch) from Lake Balaton;
and goose liver, duck, and veal
specialties. Lake Balaton is the

major source of fish in Hungary, particularly for *süllő*, a kind of perch. Hungarians are also very fond of carp (*ponty*), catfish (*harcsa*), and eel (*angolna*), which are usually stewed in a garlic-and-tomato sauce.

Portions are large, so don't plan to eat more than one main Hungarian meal a day. Desserts are lavish, and every inn seems to have its house *torta* (cake), though *rétes* (strudels), *Somlói galuska* (a steamed sponge cake soaked in chocolate sauce and whipped cream), and *palacsinta* (stuffed crepes) are ubiquitous. Traditional *rétes* fillings are *mák* (sugary poppy seeds), *meggy* (sour cherry), and *túró* (sweetened cottage cheese); palacsintas always come rolled with *dió* (sweet ground walnuts), túró, or *lekvár* (jam)—usually *barack* (apricot).

Folk Art
Hungary's centuries-old traditions of handmade, often regionally specific folk art are still beautifully alive. Intricately carved wooden boxes, vibrantly colorful embroidered tablecloths and shirts, matte-black pottery pitchers, delicately woven lace collars, ceramic plates splashed with painted flowers and birds, and decorative heavy leather whips are among the favorite handcrafted pieces a visitor can purchase. You can purchase them directly from the artisans at crafts fairs and from peddlers on the streets. Dolls

dressed in national costume are also popular souvenirs.

Lodging
Many of the major luxury and business-class hotel chains are represented in Budapest; however, all of them are Hungarian-run franchise operations with native touches that you won't find in any other Hilton or Marriott. Guest houses, also called *panziók* (pensions), provide simple accommodations—well suited to people on a budget. Like B&Bs, most are run by couples or families and offer simple breakfast facilities and usually have private bathrooms; they're generally outside the city or town center. Arrangements can be made directly with the panzió or through local tourist offices and travel agents abroad. Another good budget option is renting a room in a private home. Reservations and referrals can also be made by any tourist office.

Porcelain
Among the most sought-after items in Hungary are the exquisite hand-painted Herend and Zsolnay porcelain. Unfortunately, the prices on all makes of porcelain have risen considerably in the last few years. For guaranteed authenticity, make your purchases at the Herend and Zsolnay stores in Budapest.

Spas and Thermal Baths
Several thousand years ago, the first settlers of the area that is now

Budapest chose their home because of its abundance of hot springs. Centuries later, the Romans and the Turks built baths and developed cultures based on medicinal bathing. Now there are more than 1,000 medicinal hot springs bubbling up around the country. Budapest alone has some 14 historic working baths, which attract ailing patients with medical prescriptions for specific water cures as well as "recreational" bathers—locals and tourists alike—wanting to soak in the relaxing waters, try some of the many massages and treatments, and experience the architectural beauty of the bathhouses themselves.

For most, a visit to a bath involves soaking in several thermal pools of varying temperatures and curative contents—perhaps throwing in a game of aquatic chess—relaxing in a steam room or sauna, and getting a brisk, if not brutal, massage (average cost: 200 Ft. for a half hour). Many bath facilities are single-sex or have certain days set aside for men or women only, and most people walk around nude or with miniature loincloths, provided at the door. Men should be aware that some men-only baths have a strong gay clientele.

In addition to the ancient beauties there are newer, modern baths open to the public at many spa hotels. They lack the charm and aesthetic appeal of their older peers but provide the latest treatments in sparkling facilities. For more information, page through the "Hungary: Land of Spas" brochure published by the Hungarian Tourist Board, available free from most tourist offices.

Wine, Beer, and Spirits

Hungary tempts wine connoisseurs with its important wine regions, especially Villány, near Pécs, in the south; Eger and Tokaj in the north; and the northern shore of Lake Balaton.

Kéknyelű, Szürkebarát, and especially Olaszrizling are all common white table wines; Tokay, one of the great wines of the world, can be heavy, dark, and sweet, and is generally drunk as an aperitif or a dessert wine. It's expensive, especially by Hungarian standards, so it's usually reserved for special occasions. The gourmet red table wine of Hungary, Egri Bikavér (Bull's Blood of Eger, usually with *el toro* himself on the label), is the best buy and the safest bet with all foods.

Before- and after-dinner drinks tend toward schnapps, most notably *Barack-pálinka,* an apricot brandy. A plum brandy called *Kosher szilva-pálinka,* bottled under rabbinical supervision, is very chic. Unicum, Hungary's national liqueur, is a dark, thick, vaguely minty, and quite potent drink that could be likened to Germany's Jägermeister. Its chubby green bottle makes it a good souvenir to take home.

Major Hungarian beers are Köbányai, Dreher, Aranyhordó, Balaton Világos, and Aszok.

Quick Tours

If you're here for just a short period you need to plan carefully so as to make the most of your time in Budapest. The following itineraries outline major sights throughout the city, and will help you structure your visit efficiently. Each is intended to take about four hours—a perfect way to fill a free morning or afternoon. For more information about individual sights, *see* Chapter 2.

Várhegy (Castle Hill)

Buda's **Várhegy** district is a must-see on even the shortest itinerary. Spend the day strolling its cobblestone streets, stopping to view exhibits at the **Nemzeti Galéria** (National Gallery) or any other museum in the **Királyi palota** (Royal Palace) complex. After visiting the magnificent **Mátyás templom** (Matthias Church), walk behind it to the **Halászbástya** (Fisherman's Bastion) and indulge in the postcard Danube views framed in the Halászbástya's cheerful white stone arches.

Sights and Soaks: Buda

Climb the winding foot path to the top of **Gellért Hill** (roughly a half-hour walk), stopping for a close-up view of the massive **Szabadság szobor** (Liberation Monument) that presides over the Danube's Buda bank. Stroll along the stone walls of the **Citadella**, taking in the sweeping vistas over the Danube and Pest. Hike back down to the foot of the hill and reward your efforts with a therapeutic soak in the ornate thermal baths of Hungary's most famous spa hotel, the **Gellért Hotel.**

Sights and Soaks: Pest

Start at **Hősök tere** (Heroes' Square), taking in exhibits at the **Szépművészeti Múzeum** (Museum of Fine Arts) and/or the **Műcsarnok** (Palace of Exhibitions), strolling through the grounds of the **Vajdahunyad Vár** (Vajdahunyad Castle), then walking farther into **Városliget** (City Park) to the elegant old **Széchenyi Fürdő** (Széchenyi Baths), where you can end your tour in any of its warm bubbling pools.

Váci utca and the Danube

A leisurely few hours of strolling and shopping can begin with a pastry and espresso at Gerbeaud on **Vörösmarty tér.** From here, you can walk out to the **Korsó** and promenade along the Danube for quintessential views of Castle and Gellért hills. Double back to Vörösmarty tér and make your way down Budapest's most touristy street, **Váci utca,** a pedestrian-only zone lined with souvenir shops and expensive boutiques. At the downriver end of Váci utca is the cavernous **Vásárcsarnok** (Central Market

Hall), where you can browse through dried paprika chains and salamis.

Andrássy út and the Operaház (Opera House)

Start by visiting the **Szent István Bazilika** (St. Stephen's Basilica) and the **Nagy Zsinagóga** (Great Synagogue), about a 10-minute walk from each other. Then head over to the base of **Andrássy út** and begin walking to its other end, at **Hősök tere.** Without any pauses,

the walk would take about 45 minutes, but you'll want to stop along the way—to admire the **Operaház** (Opera House) and to have a cappuccino at the Művész café, whose outdoor tables are perfect for people-watching. If you're interested in taking a 50-minute guided tour of the Opera House, plan on arriving around 3 or 4 PM. At Heroes' Square, you can visit both the **Szépművészeti Múzeum** and the **Műcsarnok.**

2 Exploring Budapest

THE PRINCIPAL SIGHTS of Budapest fall roughly into three areas, each of which can be comfortably covered on foot. The Budapest hills are best explored by public transportation. Note that street names have been changed in the past several years to purge all reminders of the Communist regime. Underneath the new names, the old ones remain, canceled out by a big red slash. Also note that a Roman-numeral prefix listed before an address refers to one of Budapest's 22 districts.

Numbers in the text correspond to numbers in the margin and on the Várhegy (Castle Hill) and Exploring Budapest maps.

Várhegy (Castle Hill)

Most of the major sights of Buda are on Várhegy (Castle Hill), a long, narrow plateau laced with cobblestone streets, clustered with beautifully preserved Baroque, Gothic, and Renaissance houses, and crowned by the magnificent Royal Palace. The area is theoretically banned to private cars (except for those of neighborhood residents and Hilton Hotel guests), but the streets manage to be lined bumper to bumper with Trabants and Mercedes all the same—sometimes the only visual element to verify you're not in a fairy tale. As in all of Budapest, thriving urban new has taken up residence in historic old; international corporate offices, diplomatic residences, restaurants, and boutiques occupy many of its landmark buildings. But these are still the exceptions, as most flats and homes are lived in by private families. The most striking example, perhaps, is the Hilton Hotel on Hess András tér, which has ingeniously incorporated remains of Castle Hill's oldest church (a tower and one wall), built by Dominican friars in the 13th century.

A GOOD WALK

Castle Hill's cobblestone streets and numerous museums are made to be explored on foot: Plan to spend about a day here. Most of the transportation options for getting to Castle Hill deposit you on Szent György tér or Dísz tér. It's impossible not to find Castle Hill, but it is possible to be confused about how to get on top of it. If you're already

on the Buda side of the river, you can take the Castle bus—
Várbusz—from the Moszkva tér metro station, northwest
of Castle Hill. If you're starting out from Pest, you can take
a taxi or Bus 16 from Erzsébet tér or, the most scenic al-
ternative, cross the Széchenyi Lánchíd (Chain Bridge) on
foot to Clark Ádám tér and ride the *Sikló* (funicular rail)
up Castle Hill (☞ Clark Ádám tér, *below*).

Begin your exploration by walking slightly farther south
to visit the **Királyi Palota** at the southern end of the hill.
Of the palace's several major museums, the **Magyar Nemzeti
Galéria** ② and the **Budapesti Történeti Múzeum** ③ are particularly interesting. From here, you can cover the rest of
the area by walking north along its handful of charming
streets. From Dísz tér, start with Tárnok utca, whose houses
and usually open courtyards offer glimpses of how Hungarians have integrated contemporary life into Gothic, Renaissance, and Baroque settings; of particular interest are
the houses at No. 16, now the Arany Hordo restaurant, and
at No. 18, the 15th-century Arany Sas Patika (Golden
Eagle Pharmacy Museum), with a naïf Madonna and child
in an overhead niche. This tiny museum displays instruments,
prescriptions, books, and other artifacts from 16th- and 17th-
century pharmacies. Modern commerce is also integrated
into Tárnok utca's historic homes; you'll encounter numerous folk souvenir shops and tiny boutiques lining the
street. Tárnok utca funnels into Szentháromság tér, home
of **Mátyás templom** ⑦ and behind it, the **Halászbástya** ⑧.

After exploring them, double back to Dísz tér and set out
northward again on Úri utca, which runs parallel to Tárnok
utca; this long street is lined with beautiful, genteel homes.
The funny little Telefónia Museum, at No. 49, is worth a
stop, as is the **Budavári Labirintus** ⑥, at No. 9. At the end
of Úri utca you'll reach **Kapisztrán tér** ⑬. From here, you
can walk south again on a parallel street, Országház utca
(Parliament Street), the main thoroughfare of 18th-century
Buda; it takes its name from the building at No. 28, which
was the seat of Parliament from 1790 to 1807. You'll end
up back at Szentháromság tér, with just two streets remaining to explore.

You can stroll down charming little Fortuna utca, named for the 18th-century Fortuna Inn, which now houses the **Magyar Kereskedelmi és Vendéglátóipari Múzeum** ⑨. At the end of Fortuna utca you'll reach **Bécsi kapu tér** ⑫, opening to Moszkva tér just below. Go back south on the last of the district's streets, Táncsics Mihály utca, stopping at the **Középkori Zsidó Imaház** ⑪ and the **Zenetörténeti Múzeum** ⑩. Next door, at No. 9, is the Baroque house (formerly the Royal Mint) where rebel writer Tancsics Mihály was imprisoned in the dungeons and freed by the people on the Day of Revolution, March 15, 1848. You'll find yourself in front of the Hilton Hotel, back at Hess András tér, bordering Szentháromság tér. Those whose feet haven't protested yet can finish off their tour of Castle Hill by doubling back to the northern end and strolling south back to Dísz tér on **Tóth Árpád sétány,** the romantic, tree-lined promenade along the Buda side of the hill.

TIMING

Castle Hill is small enough to cover in one day, but perusing its major museums and several tiny exhibits will require more time.

SIGHTS TO SEE

⑫ **Bécsi kapu tér** (Vienna Gate Square). Marking the northern entrance to Castle Hill, the stone gateway (rebuilt in 1936) called Vienna Gate opens toward Vienna—or, closer at hand, Moszkva tér just below. The square named after it has some fine Baroque and rococo houses but is dominated by the enormous neo-Romanesque (1913–1917) headquarters of the **Országos Levéltár** (Hungarian National Archives), which resembles a cathedral-like shrine to paperwork.

❸ **Budapesti Történeti Múzeum** (Budapest History Museum). The palace's Baroque southern wing (E) contains the Budapest History Museum, displaying a fascinating permanent exhibit of modern Budapest history from Buda's liberation from the Turks in 1686 through the 1970s. Viewing the vintage 19th- and 20th-century photos and videos of the castle, the Széchenyi Lánchíd, and other Budapest monuments—and seeing them as the backdrop to the horrors of World War II and the 1956 Revolution—helps to put your later sightseeing in context; while you're browsing, peek out one of the windows overlooking the Danube and Pest and let it start seeping in.

Through historical documents, objects, and art, other permanent exhibits depict the medieval history of the Buda fortress and the capital as a whole. This is the best place to view remains of the medieval Royal Palace and other archaeological excavations. Some of the artifacts unearthed during excavations are in the vestibule in the basement; others are still among the remains of medieval structures. Down in the cellars are the original medieval vaults of the palace; portraits of King Matthias and his second wife, Beatrice of Aragon; and many late-14th-century statues that probably adorned the Renaissance palace. ⊠ *Royal Palace (Wing E), Szt. György tér 2,* ☎ *1/375–7533.* ☎ *270 Ft.* ☉ *Mar.–mid-May and mid-Sept.–Oct., Wed.–Mon. 10–6; mid-May–mid-Sept., daily 10–6; Nov.–Feb., Wed.–Mon. 10–4.*

❻ Budavári Labirintus (Labyrinth of Buda Castle). Used as a wine cellar during the 16th and 17th centuries and then as an air-raid shelter during World War II, the labyrinth—entered at Úri utca 9 below an early 18th-century house—can be explored with a tour or, if you dare, on your own. There are some English-language brochures available. ⊠ *Úri utca 9,* ☎ *1/375–6858.* ☎ *750 Ft.* ☉ *Daily 9:30–7:30.*

❹ Hadtörténeti Múzeum (Museum of Military History). Fittingly, this museum is lodged in a former barracks, on the northwestern corner of Kapisztrán tér. The exhibits, which include collections of uniforms and military regalia, trace the military history of Hungary from the original Magyar conquest in the 9th century through the period of Ottoman rule to the middle of this century. You can arrange an English-language tour in advance for around 1,000 forints. ⊠ *I, Tóth Árpád sétány 40,* ☎ *1/356–9522.* ☎ *270 Ft.* ☉ *Apr.–Sept., Tues.–Sun. 10–6; Oct.–Mar., Tues.–Sun. 10–4.*

★ ❽ Halászbástya (Fishermen's Bastion). The wondrous porch overlooking the Danube and Pest is the neo-Romanesque Fishermen's Bastion, a merry cluster of white stone towers, arches, and columns above a modern bronze statue of St. Stephen, Hungary's first king. Medieval fishwives once peddled their wares here, but the site is now home to souvenirs, crafts, and music.

12

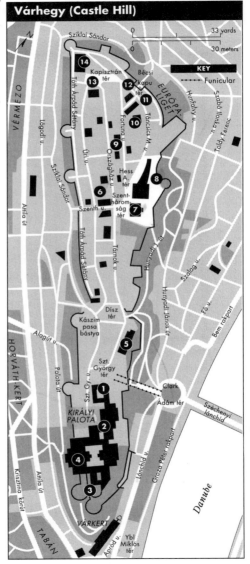

Várhegy (Castle Hill)

⑬ Kapisztrán tér (Capistrano Square). Castle Hill's north-ernmost square was named after St. John of Capistrano, an Italian friar who in 1456 recruited a crusading army to fight the Turks who were threatening Hungary. There's a statue of this honored Franciscan on the northwest corner; also here are the **Museum of Military History** (☞ *above*) and the remains of the 12th-century Gothic **Mária Mag-dolna templom** (Church of St. Mary Magdalene). Its *torony* (tower), completed in 1496, is the only part left standing; the rest of the church was destroyed by air raids during World War II.

★ Királyi Palota (Royal Palace, commonly called Buda Cas-tle). During a seven-week siege at the end of 1944, the en-tire Castle Hill district of palaces, mansions, and churches was turned into one vast ruin. The final German stand was in the Royal Palace, which was utterly gutted by fire; by the end of the siege its walls were reduced to rubble, and just a few scarred pillars and blackened statues protruded from the wreckage. The destruction was incalculable, yet it gave archaeologists and art historians an opportunity to discover the medieval buildings that once stood on the site of this Baroque and neo-Baroque palace. Fortunately, de-tails of the edifices of the kings of the Árpád and Anjou dy-nasties, of the Holy Roman Emperor Sigismund, and of the great 15th-century king Mátthiás Corvinus had been pre-served in some 80 medieval reports, travelogues, books, and itineraries that were subsequently used to reconstruct the complex.

The postwar rebuilding was slow and painstaking. In some places debris more than 20 ft deep had to be removed; the remains found on the medieval levels were restored to their original planes. Freed from mounds of rubble, the foundation walls and medieval castle walls were completed, and the ramparts surrounding the medieval royal residence were re-created as close to their original shape and size as possi-ble. Out of this herculean labor emerged the Royal Palace of today, a vast cultural center and museum complex (☞ Budapesti Történeti Múzeum, *above; and* Ludwig Múzeum, Magyar Nemzeti Galéria, *and* Országos Széchenyi Könyvtár, *below*).

⓫ Középkori Zsidó Imaház (Medieval Synagogue). The excavated one-room Medieval Synagogue is now used as a museum. On display are objects relating to the Jewish community, including religious inscriptions, frescoes, and tombstones dating to the 15th century. ✉ *Táncsics Mihály u. 26,* ☎ *1/355–8849.* 🎟 *120 Ft.* ☼ *May–Oct., Tues.–Fri. 10–2, weekends 10–6.*

❶ Ludwig Múzeum This collection of more than 200 pieces of Hungarian and contemporary international art, including works by Picasso and Lichtenstein, occupies the castle's northern wing. ✉ *Royal Palace (Wing A), Dísz tér 17,* ☎ *1/375–7533.* 🎟 *120 Ft., free Tues.* ☼ *Tues.–Sun. 10–6.*

❾ Magyar Kereskedelmi és Vendéglátóipari Múzeum (Hungarian Museum of Commerce and Catering). The 18th-century Fortuna Inn now serves visitors in a different way—as the Catering Museum. Displays in a permanent exhibit show the city as a tourist destination from 1870 to the 1930s; you can see, for example, what a room at the Gellért Hotel, still operating today, would have looked like in 1918. The Commerce Museum, just across the courtyard, chronicles the history of Hungarian commerce from the late 19th century to 1947, when the new Communist regime "liberated" the economy into socialism. The four-room exhibit includes everything from an antique chocolate-and-caramel vending machine to early shoe-polish advertisements. You can rent an English-language recorded tour for 200 Ft. ✉ *Fortuna utca 4,* ☎ *1/375–6249.* 🎟 *120 Ft., free Fri.* ☼ *Wed.–Fri. 10–5, weekends 10–6.*

❷ Magyar Nemzeti Galéria (Hungarian National Gallery). The immense center block of the Royal Palace (made up of Wings B, C, and D) exhibits a wide range of Hungarian fine art, from medieval ecclesiastical paintings and statues, through Gothic, Renaissance, and Baroque art, to a rich collection of 19th- and 20th-century works. Especially notable are the works of the romantic painter Mihály Munkácsy, the impressionist Pál Szinyei Merse, and the surrealist Kosztka Csontváry, whom Picasso much admired. There is also a large collection of modern Hungarian sculpture. There are labels and commentary in English for both permanent and temporary exhibits. If you contact the museum in advance, you can book a tour for up to five people with an English-speaking guide. ✉ *Royal Palace (entrance in Wing C), Dísz tér 17,* ☎ *1/375–7533.* 🎫 *Gallery 220 Ft., tour 1,000 Ft.* ☉ *Mid-Mar.–Oct., Tues.–Sun. 10–6; Nov.–mid-Mar., Tues.–Sun. 10–4. (Note: Mid-Jan.–mid-Mar. hrs. may be reduced to Fri.–Sun. only, 10–4).*

★ **➐ Mátyás templom** (Matthias Church). The Gothic Matthias Church is officially the Buda Church of Our Lady but better known by the name of the 15th century's "just king" of Hungary, who was married here twice. It is sometimes called the Coronation Church, because the last two kings of Hungary were crowned here: the Hapsburg emperor Franz Joseph in 1867 and his grandnephew Karl IV in 1916. Originally built for the city's German population in the mid-13th century, the church has endured many alterations and assaults. For almost 150 years it was the main mosque of the Turkish overlords—and the predominant impact of its festive pillars is decidedly Byzantine. Badly damaged during the recapture of Buda in 1686, it was completely rebuilt between 1873 and 1896 by Frigyes Schulek, who gave it an asymmetrical western front, with one high and one low spire, and a fine rose window; the south porch is from the 14th century.

The **Szentháromság Kápolna** (Trinity Chapel) holds an *encolpion,* an enameled casket containing a miniature copy of the Gospel to be worn on the chest; it belonged to the 12th-century king Béla III and his wife, Anne of Chatillon. Their burial crowns and a cross, scepter, and rings found in their excavated graves are also displayed here. The church's **treasury** contains Renaissance and Baroque chalices, monstrances, and vestments. High Mass is celebrated every Sunday at 10 AM with full orchestra and choir—and often with major soloists; get here early if you want a seat. During the summer there are usually organ recitals on Friday at 8 PM. Tourists are asked to remain at the back of the church during weddings and services (it's least intrusive to come after 9:30 AM weekdays and between 1 and 5 PM Sundays and holidays). ✉ *I, Szentháromság tér 2,* ☎ *1/355–5657.* ☉ *Daily 7 AM–8 PM.* 🎫 *Church free, except during concerts; treasury 100 Ft.* ☉ *Treasury daily 9:30–5:30.*

➍ Országos Széchenyi Könyvtár (Széchenyi National Library). The western wing (F) of the Royal Palace is home to the Na-

tional Library, which houses more than 2 million volumes.
Its archives include well-preserved medieval codices,
manuscripts, and historic correspondence. This is not a
lending library, but the reading rooms are open to the public (though you must show a passport), and even the most
valuable materials can be viewed on microfilm. Small, temporary exhibits on rare books and documents are usually
on display; the hours and admission fees for these are quite
variable. Note that the entire library closes for one month
every summer, usually in July or August. ⊠ *Royal Palace
(Wing F). To arrange a tour with an English-speaking guide,*
☎ *1/375–7533.* ⊡ *300 Ft.* ☉ *Reading rooms Mon. 1–9,
Tues.–Sat. 9–9; exhibits Mon. 1–6, Tues.–Sat. 10–6.*

Statue of Prince Eugene of Savoy. In front of the Royal
Palace, facing the Danube by the entrance to Wing C,
stands an equestrian statue of Prince Eugene of Savoy, a commander of the army that liberated Hungary from the Turks
at the end of the 17th century. From here there is a superb
view across the river to Pest.

Szentháromság tér (Holy Trinity Square). This square is
named for its Baroque **Trinity Column,** erected in 1712–
1713 as a gesture of thanksgiving by survivors of a plague.
The column stands in front of the famous Gothic Matthias
Church (☞ *above*), its large pedestal a perfect seat from which
to watch the wedding spectacles that take over the church
on spring and summer weekends: From morning till night,
frilly engaged pairs flow in one after the other and, after a
brief transformation inside, back out onto the square.

★ **Tóth Árpád sétány.** This romantic, tree-lined promenade
along the Buda side of the hill is often mistakenly overlooked
by sightseers. Beginning at the Museum of Military History (☞ *above*) the promenade takes you "behind the
scenes" along the back sides of the matte-pastel Baroque
houses you saw on Úri utca, with their regal arched windows and wrought-iron gates. On a late spring afternoon,
the fragrance of the cherry trees may be enough to revive
even the most weary.

Úri utca. Running parallel to Tárnok utca, Úri utca has been
less commercialized by boutiques and other shops; the
longest and oldest street in the castle district, it is lined with

many stately houses, all worth special attention for their delicately carved details. Both gateways of the Baroque palace at **Nos. 48–50** are articulated by Gothic niches. The **Telefónia Múzeum** (Telephone Museum), at No. 49, is an endearing little museum entered through a central court-yard shared with the local district police station. Although vintage telephone systems are still in use all over the coun-try, both the oldest and most recent products of telecom-munication—from the 1882 wooden box with hose attachment to the latest, slickest fax machines—can be ob-served and tested here. *Telefónia Múzeum:* ⊠ *Úri utca 49,* ☎ *1/201–8188.* ⌑ *60 Ft.* ☉ *Nov.–Apr., Tues.–Sun. 10–4; May–Oct., Tues.–Sun. 10–6.*

❺ Várszínház (Castle Theater). Once a Franciscan church, this was transformed into a more secular royal venue in 1787 under the supervision of courtier Farkas Kempelen. The first theatrical performance in Hungarian was held here in 1790. Heavily damaged during World War II, the theater was re-built and reopened in 1978. While the building retains its original late-Baroque-style facade, the interior was reno-vated with marble and concrete. It is now used as the stu-dio theater of the National Theater and occasionally for classical recitals, and there is usually a historical exhibition in its foyer—usually theater-related, such as a display of cos-tumes. ⊠ *Színház utca 1–3,* ☎ *1/375–8011.*

❿ Zenetörténeti Múzeum (Museum of Music History). This handsome gray-and-pearl-stone 18th-century palace is where Beethoven allegedly stayed in 1800 when he came to Buda to conduct his works. Now a museum, it displays rare manuscripts and old instruments downstairs in its per-manent collection and temporary exhibits upstairs in a small, sunlit hall. The museum also often hosts intimate clas-sical recitals. ⊠ *Táncsics Mihály u. 7,* ☎ *1/214–6770.* ⌑ *170 Ft.* ☉ *Mid-Nov.–late-Dec. and first 2 wks of Mar., Tues.–Sun. 10–5; mid-Mar.–mid-Nov., Tues.–Sun. 10–6.*

Tabán and Gellért-hegy (Tabán and Gellért Hill)

Spreading below Castle Hill is the old quarter called the Tabán (from the Turkish word for "armory"). A onetime suburb of Buda, it was known at the end of the 17th century as Little Serbia (*Rác*) because so many Serbian refugees settled here after fleeing from the Turks. It later became a district of vineyards and small taverns. Though most of the small houses characteristic of this district have been demolished—mainly in the interest of easing traffic—a few picturesque buildings remain.

Gellért-hegy (Gellért Hill), 761 ft high, is the most beautiful natural formation on the Buda bank. It takes its name from St. Gellért (Gerard) of Csanad, a Venetian bishop who came to Hungary in the 11th century and was supposedly flung to his death from the top of the hill by pagans. The walk up can be tough, but take solace from the cluster of hot springs at the foot of the hill, which soothe and cure bathers at the Rác, Rudas, and Gellért baths.

A GOOD WALK

From the **Semmelweis Orvostörténeti Múzeum** ⑮, walk around the corner to Szarvas tér and a few yards toward the river to the **Tabán plébánia-templom** ⑯. Walking south on Attila út and crossing to the other side of Hegyalja út, you'll be at the foot of Gellért Hill. From here, take a deep breath and climb the paths and stairs to the **Citadella** ⑳ fortress at the top of the hill (about 30 minutes). After taking in the views and exploring the area, you can descend and treat yourself to a soak or a swim at the **Gellért Szálloda és Thermál Fürdő** ⑲ at the southeastern foot of the hill. On foot, take the paths down the southeastern side of the hill. You can also take Bus 27 down the back of the hill to Móricz Zsigmond körtér and walk back toward the Gellért on busy Bartók Béla út, or take Tram 47, 49, 18, or 19 a couple of stops to Szent Gellért tér.

TIMING

The Citadella and Szabadság Szobor are lit in golden lights every night, but the entire Gellért-hegy is at its scenic best every year on August 20, when it forms the backdrop to the spectacular St. Stephen's Day fireworks display.

SIGHTS TO SEE

★ ⑳ **Citadella.** The fortress atop the hill was a much-hated sight for Hungarians. They called it the Gellért Bastille, for it was erected, on the site of an earlier wooden observatory, by the Austrian army as a lookout after the 1848–1849 War of Independence. But no matter what its history may be, the views from this ring of walls are breathtaking. Its transformation into a tourist site during the 1960s improved its image, with the addition of cafés, a beer garden, wine cellars, and a hostel. In its inner wall is a small graphic exhibition (with some relics) of Budapest's 2,000-year history. ☎ *No phone.* ☞ *Free.* ☉ *Accessible at all times.*

Erzsébethíd (Elizabeth Bridge). This bridge was named for Empress Elizabeth (1837–1898), called Sissi, of whom the Hungarians were particularly fond. The beautiful but unhappy wife of Franz Joseph, she was stabbed to death in 1898 by an anarchist while boarding a boat on Lake Geneva. The original bridge was built between 1897 and 1903; at the time, it was the longest single-span suspension bridge in Europe. It was destroyed by the Germans in 1945 and its modern replacement dates from 1964.

★ ⑲ **Gellért Szálloda és Thermál Fürdő** (Gellért Hotel and Thermal Baths). At the foot of the Gellért Hill are these beautiful art-nouveau establishments. The Danubius Hotel Gellért (☞ Chapter 4) is the oldest spa hotel in Hungary, with hot springs that have supplied curative baths for nearly 2,000 years. It is the most popular among tourists, as you don't need reservations, it's quite easy to communicate, and there's a wealth of treatments—including chamomile steam baths, salt-vapor inhalations, and hot mud packs. Many of these treatments require a doctor's prescription; they will accept prescriptions from foreign doctors. Men and women have separate steam and sauna rooms; both the indoor pool and the outdoor wave pool are coed. ✉ *XI, Gellért tér 1,* ☎ *1/385–3555 (baths).* ☞ *Indoor baths and steam rooms 500 Ft. per 1½ hrs; indoor pool 1,300 Ft. per day.* ☉ *Baths weekdays 6 AM–6 PM, weekends 6:30 AM–1 PM (May–Sept. until 4 PM). May–Sept. weekend massage only until 1 PM. Wave pool May–Sept., daily 6 AM–6 PM.*

⑰ **Rác Fürdő** (Rác Baths). The bright-yellow building tucked away at the foot of Gellért Hill near the Elizabeth Bridge houses these baths, built during the reign of King Zsigmond in the early 15th century and rebuilt by Miklós Ybl in the

20

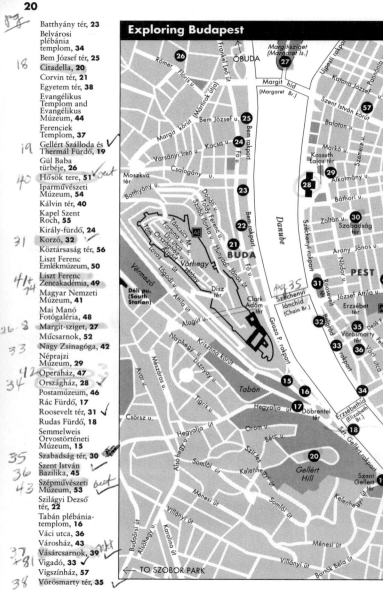

Exploring Budapest

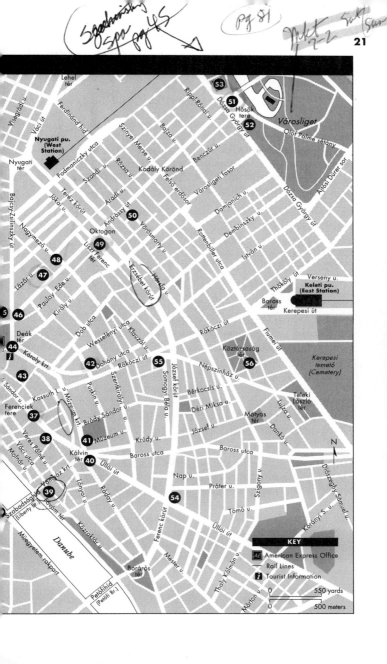

mid-19th century. Its waters contain alkaline salts and
other minerals; you can also get a massage. Women can bathe
on Monday, Wednesday, and Friday; men on Tuesday,
Thursday, and Saturday. These baths are particularly popular with the gay community. ☒ *I, Hadnagy utca 8–10,*
☎ *1/356–1322.* ☜ *450 Ft.* ☾ *Mon.–Sat. 6:30 AM–6 PM.*

⑱ Rudas Fürdő (Rudas Baths). This bath is on the riverbank,
the original Turkish pool making its interior possibly the
most dramatically beautiful of Budapest's baths. A high,
domed roof admits pinpricks of bluish-green light into the
dark, circular stone hall with its austere columns and
arches. Fed by eight springs with a year-round temperature
of 44°C (111°F), the Rudas's highly fluoridated waters
have been known for 1,000 years. The facility is open to
men only (though it does not have a large gay following);
a less interesting outer swimming pool is open to both
sexes. Massages are available. ☒ *I, Döbrentei tér 9,* ☎ *1/
356–1322.* ☜ *400 Ft.* ☾ *Weekdays 6 AM–6 PM, weekends
6 AM–noon.*

⑮ Semmelweis Orvostörténeti Múzeum (Semmelweis Museum of Medical History). This splendid Baroque house was
the birthplace of Ignác Semmelweis (1818–1865), the Hungarian physician who proved the contagiousness of puer-
peral (childbed) fever. It's now a museum that traces the
history of healing. Semmelweis's grave is in the garden. ☒
Apród utca 1–3, ☎ *1/375–3533.* ☜ *100 Ft.* ☾ *Tues.–Sun.
10:30–5:30.*

Szabadság Szobor (Liberation Memorial). Visible from
many parts of the city, this 130-ft-high 1947 memorial, which
starts just below the southern edge of the Citadella and towers above it, honors the 1944–1945 siege of Budapest and
the Russian soldiers who fell in the battle. It is the work of
noted Hungarian sculptor Zsigmond Kisfaludi-Stróbl, and
from the distance it looks light, airy, and even liberating.
A sturdy young girl, her hair and robe swirling in the wind,
holds a palm branch high above her head. Until recently,
she was further embellished with sculptures of giants slay-
ing dragons, Red Army soldiers, and peasants rejoicing at
the freedom that Soviet liberation promised (but failed) to
bring to Hungary. Since 1992, her mood has lightened: In
the Budapest city government's systematic purging of Com-

munist symbols, the Red Combat infantrymen who had flanked the Liberation statue for decades were hacked off and carted away. A few are now on display among the other evicted statues in the Szobor Park in the city's 22nd district (☞ *below*). ⊠ *Gellért-hegy.*

Szarvas-ház (Stag House). This Louis XVI–style building is named for the former Szarvas Café or, more accurately, for its extant trade sign, with an emblem of a stag not quite at bay, which can be seen above the triangular arched entryway. For years, the structure housed the Arany Szarvas restaurant, which preserved some of the mood of the old Tabán, but at press time it was closed for renovations and seemed likely to change hands and reopen as something else. ⊠ *Szarvas tér 1.*

Szobor Park (Statue Park). For a look at Budapest's too-recent Iron Curtain past, make the 30-minute trip out to this open-air exhibit, cleverly nicknamed "Tons of Socialism," where 42 of the Communist statues and memorials that once dominated the city's streets and squares have been put out to pasture since the political changes in 1989. Here you can wander among mammoth Lenin and Marx statues and buy socialist-nostalgia souvenirs while songs from the Hungarian and Russian workers' movement play bombastically in the background. ⊠ *XXII, Balatoni út, corner of Szabadkai út,* ☎ FAX *1/227–7446.* 🖙 *250 Ft.* ☉ *Mid-Apr.–Oct., daily 8–8; Nov.–mid-Apr., weekends 10–dusk.*

🔟 **Tabán plébánia-templom** (Tabán Parish Church). In 1736, this church was built on the site of a Turkish mosque and subsequently renovated and reconstructed several times. Its present form—mustard-color stone with a rotund, green clock tower—could be described as restrained Baroque. ⊠ *I, Attila u. 1.*

North Buda

Most of these sights are along Fő utca (Main Street), a long, straight thoroughfare that starts at the Chain Bridge and runs parallel to the Danube. It is lined on both sides with multistory late-18th-century houses—many darkened by soot and showing their age more than those you've seen in sparklingly restored areas like Castle Hill. This northbound exploration can be done with the help of Bus 86, which covers the waterfront, or on foot, although distances are fairly great.

A GOOD WALK

Beginning at **Batthyány tér** ㉓, with its head-on view of Parliament across the Danube, continue north on Fő utca, passing (or stopping to bathe at) the famous Turkish **Király-fürdő** ㉔. From **Bem József tér** ㉕, one block north, turn left (away from the river) up Fekete Sas utca, crossing busy Margit körút and turning right, one block past, up Mecset utca. This will take you up the hill to **Gül Baba türbéje** ㉖.

TIMING

The tour can fit easily into a few hours, including a good hour-and-a-half soak at the baths; expect the walk from Bem József tér up the hill to Gül Baba türbéje to take about 25 minutes. Fő utca and Bem József tér can get congested during rush hours (from around 7:30 to 8:30 AM and 4:30 to 6 PM). Remember that museums are closed Mondays and that the Király Baths are open to men and women on different days of the week.

SIGHTS TO SEE

㉓ **Batthyány tér.** This lovely square, open on its river side, affords a grand view of Parliament, directly across the Danube. The M2 subway, the HÉV electric railway from Szentendre, and various suburban and local buses converge on the square, as do peddlers hawking everything from freshly picked flowers to mismatched pairs of shoes. At No. 7 Batthyány tér is the beautiful, Baroque twin-towered **Szent Anna-templom** (Church of St. Anne), dating from 1740–1762, its oval cupola adorned with frescoes and statuary.

㉕ **Bem József tér.** This square near the river is not particularly picturesque and can get heavy with traffic, but it houses the statue of its important namesake, Polish general József Bem, who offered his services to the 1848 revolutionaries in Vienna and then Hungary. Reorganizing the rebel forces in Transylvania, he was the war's most successful general. It was at this statue on October 23, 1956, that a great student demonstration in sympathy with the Poles' striving for liberal reforms exploded into the brave and tragic Hungarian uprising suppressed by the Red Army.

㉑ Corvin tér. This charming, small, shady square on Fő utca is the site of the turn-of-the-century Folk Art Institute administration building and the concert hall Budai Vigadó (☞ Chapter 5) at No. 8.

㉖ Gül Baba türbéje (Tomb of Gül Baba). Gül Baba, a 16th-century dervish and poet whose name means "father of roses" in Turkish, was buried in a tomb built of carved stone blocks with four oval windows. He fought in several wars waged by the Turks and fell during the siege of Buda in 1541. The tomb remains a place of pilgrimage; it is considered Europe's northernmost Muslim shrine and marks the spot where he was slain. Set at an elevation on Rózsadomb (Rose Hill), the tomb is near a good lookout for city views. ⊠ *Mecset utca 14,* ☎ *1/355–8764.* ⊡ *100 Ft.* ⊙ *May– Oct., Tues.–Sun. 10–4.*

☾ Gyermek vasút (Children's Railway). The 12-km (7-mi) Children's Railway runs from Széchenyihegy to Hűvösvölgy. The sweeping views make the trip well worthwhile for children and adults alike. Departures are from Széchenyihegy, which you can reach by taking a cogwheel railway. ⊠ *Cogwheel railway station: intersection of Szillágyi Erzsébet fasor and Pasaréti út.* ⊡ *140 Ft. each way.* ⊙ *Trains run mid-Jan.– late Mar. and mid-Sept.–Dec., Wed.–Sun. 8–4; mid-Jan. and Apr.–mid-Sept., Tues.–Sun. 8–5.*

Kapucinus templom (Capuchin Church). This church was converted from a Turkish mosque at the end of the 17th century. Damaged during the revolution in 1849, it acquired its current romantic-style exterior when it was rebuilt a few years later. ⊠ *Fő utca.*

㉔ Király-fürdő (King Baths). The royal gem of Turkish baths in Budapest was built in the 16th century by the Turkish pasha of Buda. Its stone cupola, crowned by a golden moon and crescent, arches over the steamy, dark pools indoors. It is open to men on Monday, Wednesday, and Friday; to women on Tuesday, Thursday, and Saturday. These baths are very popular with the gay community. ⊠ *II, Fő utca 84,* ☎ *1/202–3688.* ⊡ *400 Ft.* ⊙ *Weekdays 6:30 AM–6 PM, Sat. 6:30 AM–noon.*

㉒ **Szilágyi Dezső tér.** This is another of the charming little squares punctuating Fő utca; here you'll find the composer Béla Bartók's house, at No. 4.

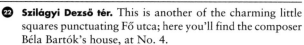

Margit-sziget (Margaret Island)

More than 2½ km (1½ mi) long and covering nearly 200 acres, **Margit-sziget** ㉗ is ideal for strolling, jogging, sunbathing, or just loafing. In good weather, the island draws a multitudinous cross section of the city's population out to its gardens and sporting facilities. The outdoor pool complex of the Palatinus Baths (toward the Buda side), built in 1921, can attract tens of thousands of people on a summer day. Nearby are a tennis stadium, a youth athletic center, boathouses, sports grounds, and, most impressive of all, the Nemzeti Sportuszoda (National Sports Swimming Pool), designed by the architect Alfred Hajós (while still in his teens, Hajós won two gold medals in swimming at the first modern Olympic Games, held in Athens in 1896). In addition, walkers, joggers, bicyclists, and rollerbladers do laps around the island's perimeter and up and down the main road, closed to traffic except for Bus 26 (and a few official vehicles), which travels up and down the island and across the Margaret Bridge to and from Pest.

The island's natural curative hot springs have given rise to the Danubius Grand and Thermal hotels on the northern end of the island (☞ Chapter 4) and are piped in to two spa hotels on the mainland, the Aquincum on the Buda bank and the Hélia on the Pest side.

A GOOD WALK

Entering the island from its southern end at the **Margit-híd,** stroll (or rent a bicycle and pedal) north along any of the several tree-shaded paths, including the **Művész sétány,** pausing for a picnic on an open lawn, and eventually ending up at the rock garden at the northern end. From here, you can wander back to the southern end or take Bus 26 on the island's only road.

TIMING

A leisurely walk simply from one end to the other would take about 40 minutes, but it's nice to spend extra time wandering. To experience Margaret Island's role in Budapest life fully, go on a Saturday or Sunday afternoon to join and/or watch people whiling away the day. Sunday is a particularly good choice for strategic sightseers, who can utilize the rest of the week to cover those city sights and areas that are closed on Sundays. On weekdays, you'll share the island only with joggers and kids playing hooky from school.

SIGHTS TO SEE

Margit-híd (Margaret Bridge). At the southern end of the island, the Margaret Bridge is the closer of the two entrances for those coming from downtown Buda or Pest. Just north of the Chain Bridge, the bridge walkway provides gorgeous midriver views of Castle Hill and Parliament. Toward the end of 1944, the bridge was blown up by the retreating Nazis while it was crowded with rush-hour traffic. It was rebuilt in the same unusual shape—forming an obtuse angle in midstream, with a short leg leading down to the island. The original bridge was built during the 1840s by French engineer Ernest Gouin in collaboration with Gustave Eiffel.

㉗ Margit-sziget (Margaret Island). The island was first mentioned almost 2,000 years ago as the summer residence of the commander of the Roman garrison at nearby Aquincum. Later known as Rabbit Island (Insula Leporum), it was a royal hunting ground during the Árpád dynasty. King Imre, who reigned from 1196 to 1204, held court here, and several convents and monasteries were built here during the Middle Ages. (During a walk round the island, you'll see the ruins of a few of these buildings.) It takes its current name from St. Margaret, the pious daughter of King Béla IV, who at the ripe old age of 10 retired to a Dominican nunnery here.

㋡ Margit-sziget Vadaspark (Margaret Island Game Park). Just east of the rose garden is a small would-be petting zoo, if the animals were allowed to be petted. A fenced-in compound houses a menagerie of goats, rabbits, donkeys, assorted fowl and ducks, and gargantuan peacocks that sit heavily on straining tree branches. ▱ *Free.*

Marosvásárhelyi zenélő kút (Marosvásárhely Musical Fountain). At the northern end of the island is a copy of the water-powered Marosvásárhely Musical Fountain, which plays songs and chimes. The original was designed more than 150 years ago by a Transylvanian named Péter Bodor. It stands near a picturesque, artificial **rock garden** with Japanese dwarf trees and lily ponds. The stream coursing through it never freezes, for it comes from a natural hot spring causing it instead to give off thick steam in winter that enshrouds the garden in a mystical cloud.

Művész sétány (Artists' Promenade). Through the center of the island runs the Artists' Promenade, lined with busts of Hungarian artists, writers, and musicians. Shaded by giant plane trees, it's a perfect place to stroll. The promenade passes close to the **rose garden** (in the center of the island), a large grassy lawn surrounded by blooming flower beds planted with hundreds of kinds of flowers. It's a great spot to picnic or to watch a game of soccer or Ultimate Frisbee, both of which are regularly played here on weekend afternoons.

Downtown Pest and the Kis körút (Little Ring Road)

Budapest's urban heart is full of bona fide sights plus innumerable tiny streets and grand avenues where you can wander for hours admiring the city's stately old buildings—some freshly sparkling after their first painting in decades, others silently but still elegantly crumbling.

Dominated by the Parliament building, the district surrounding Kossuth tér is the legislative, diplomatic, and administrative nexus of Budapest; most of the ministries are here, as are the National Bank and Courts of Justice. Downriver, the romantic Danube promenade, the Duna Korzó, extends along the stretch of riverfront across from Castle Hill. With Vörösmarty tér and pedestrian shopping street Váci utca just inland, this area forms Pest's tourist core. Going south, the Korzó ends at Március 15 tér. One block in from the river, Ferenciek tere marks the beginning of the university area, spreading south of Kossuth Lajos utca. Here, the streets are narrower and your footsteps echo off of the elegantly aging stone buildings.

Pest is laid out in broad circular *körúts* ("ring roads" or boulevards). Vámház körút is the first sector of the 2½-km (1½-mi) Kis körút (Little Ring Road), which traces the route of the Old Town wall from Szabadsághíd (Liberty Bridge) to Deák tér. Construction of the inner körút began in 1872 and was completed in 1880. Changing names as it curves, after Kálvin tér it becomes Múzeum körút (passing by the National Museum), and then Károly körút for its final stretch ending at Deák tér. Deák tér, the only place where all three subway lines converge, could be called the dead-center of downtown. East of the körút are the weathered streets of Budapest's former ghetto.

A GOOD WALK

Starting at Kossuth tér to see the **Országház** ㉘ and the **Néprajzi Múzeum** ㉙, it's worth walking a few blocks southeast to take in stately **Szabadság tér** ㉚ before heading back to the Danube and south to the foot of the **Széchenyi Lánchíd** at **Roosevelt tér** ㉛. As this tour involves quite a bit of walking, you may want to take Tram 2 from Kossuth tér a few stops downriver to Roosevelt tér to save your energy. While time and/or energy may not allow it just now, at some point during your visit, a walk across the Chain Bridge is a must. From Roosevelt tér go south, across the street, and join the **korzó** ㉜ along the river, strolling past the **Vigadó** ㉝ at Vigadó tér, all the way to the **Belvárosi plébánia templom** ㉞ at Március 15 tér, just under the Elizabeth Bridge. Double back up the korzó to Vigadó tér and walk in from the river on Vigadó utca to **Vörösmarty tér** ㉟.

Follow the crowds down pedestrian-only **Váci utca** ㊱, crossing busy Kossuth Lajos utca near Ferenciek tere and continuing along Váci utca's southern stretch to the **Vásárcsarnok** ㊳. Doubling back a few blocks on Váci utca, turn right onto Szerb utca and stroll past the **Szerb Ortodox templom** to the street's end at **Egyetem tér** ㊲. Here, you are going through the darker, narrower streets of this student-filled, increasingly trendy area. A detour into any of the other side streets will give you a good flavor of the area. Walking south on Kecskeméti utca, you will reach **Kálvin tér** ㊵. To save time and energy, you can also take Tram 47 or 49 from Fővám tér, in front of the Vásárcsarnok, one stop away from the Danube to Kálvin tér. Just north of Kálvin tér on Múzeum körút is the **Magyar Nemzeti Múzeum** ㊶. The **Nagy Zsinagóga** ㊷ is about ¾ km (⅓ mi) farther north along the Kis körút (Little Ring Road)—a longish walk or a short tram ride. From here, more walking along the körút, or a tram ride to the last stop, brings you to Pest's main hub, Deák tér. The **Szent István Bazilika** ㊺ is an extra but rewarding 500-yard walk north on Bajcsy-Zsilinszky út.

TIMING

This is a particularly rich part of the city; the suggested walk will take the better part of a day, including time to visit the museums, stroll on the korzó, and browse on Vaci utca—not to mention time for lunch. Keep in mind that the museums are closed on Monday.

SIGHTS TO SEE

㉞ **Belvárosi plébánia templom** (Inner City Parish Church). Dating to the 12th century, this is the oldest ecclesiastical building in Pest. It's actually built on something even older—the remains of the Contra Aquincum, a 3rd-century Roman fortress and tower, parts of which are visible next to the church. There is hardly any architectural style that cannot be found in some part or another, starting with a single Romanesque arch in its south tower. The single nave still has its original Gothic chancel and some 15th-century Gothic frescoes. Two side chapels contain beautifully carved Renaissance altarpieces and tabernacles of red marble from the early 16th century. During Budapest's years of Turkish occupation, the church served as a mosque—and this is remembered by a *mihrab,* a Muslim prayer niche. During the 18th century, the church was given two Baroque towers and its present facade. In 1808 it was enriched with a rococo pulpit, and still later a superb winged triptych was added to the main altar. From 1867 to 1875, Franz Liszt lived only a few steps away from the church, in a town house where he held regular "musical Sundays" at which Richard and Cosima Wagner were frequent guests and participants. Liszt's own musical Sunday mornings often began in this church. An admirer of its acoustics and organ, he conducted many masses here, including the first Budapest performance of his *Missa Choralis,* in 1872. ✉ *V, Március 15 tér 2,* ☎ *1/317–3322.*

㊳ **Egyetem tér** (University Square). Budapest's University of Law sits here in the heart of the city's university neighborhood. On one corner is the cool gray-and-green marble **Egyetemi Templom** (University Church), one of

Hungary's most beautiful Baroque buildings. Built between 1725 and 1742, it has an especially splendid pulpit.

44 **Evangélikus Templom and Evangélikus Múzeum** (Lutheran Church and Lutheran Museum). The neoclassical Lutheran Church sits in the center of it all on busy Deák tér. Classical concerts are regularly held here. The church's interior designer, János Krausz, flouted then-traditional church architecture by placing a single large interior beneath the huge vaulted roof structure. The adjoining school is now the Lutheran Museum, which traces the role of Protestantism in Hungarian history and contains Martin Luther's original will. ⊠ *Deák Ferenc tér 4,* ☎ *1/317–4173.* 🎟 *Museum 200 Ft.; church free (except during concerts).* ⊙ *Museum Tues.–Sun. 10–6.*

37 **Ferenciek Templom** (Franciscan church). This pale-yellow church was built in 1743. On the wall facing Kossuth Lajos utca is a bronze relief showing a scene from the devastating flood of 1838; the detail is so vivid that it almost makes you seasick. A faded arrow below the relief indicates the high-water mark of almost 4 ft. Next to it is the **Nereids Fountain,** a popular meeting place for students from the nearby Eötvös Loránd University. ⊠ *V, Ferenciek tere.*

Görög Ortodox templom (Greek Orthodox Church). Built at the end of the 18th century in late-Baroque style, the Greek Orthodox Church was remodeled a century later by Miklós Ybl, who designed the Opera House and many other important Budapest landmarks. The church retains some fine wood carvings and a dazzling array of icons by late-18th-century Serbian master Miklós Jankovich. ⊠ *V, Petőfi tér 2/b.*

40 **Kálvin tér** (Calvin Square). Calvin Square takes its name from the neoclassical Protestant church that tries to dominate this busy traffic hub; more glaringly noticeable, however, is the billboard of a giant Pepsi advertisement. The Kecskeméti Kapu, a main gate of Pest, once stood here, as well as a cattle market that was a notorious den of thieves. At the beginning of the 19th century, this was where Pest ended and the prairie began.

★ **32** **Korzó.** The neighborhood to the south of Roosevelt tér has regained much of its past elegance—if not its architectural grandeur—with the erection of the Atrium Hyatt, Inter-Continental, and Budapest Marriott luxury hotels. Traversing all three and continuing well beyond them is the riverside Korzó, a pedestrian promenade lined with park benches and appealing outdoor cafés from which one can enjoy postcard-perfect views of Gellért Hill and Castle Hill directly across the Danube. Try to take a stroll in the evening, when the views are lit up in shimmering gold.

Közgazdasági Egyetem (University of Economics). Just below the Liberty Bridge on the waterfront, the monumental neo-Renaissance building was once the Customs House. Built in 1871–1874 by Miklós Ybl, it is now also known as *közgáz,* after a stint during the Communist era as Karl Marx University. ⊠ *Fővám tér.*

㊶ Magyar Nemzeti Múzeum (Hungarian National Museum). Built between 1837 and 1847, the museum is a fine example of 19th-century classicism—simple, well proportioned, and surrounded by a large garden. In front of this building on March 15, 1848, Sándor Petőfi recited his revolutionary poem, the "National Song" ("Nemzeti dal"), and the "12 Points," a list of political demands by young Hungarians calling on the people to rise up against the Hapsburgs. Celebrations of the national holiday commemorating the failed revolution are held on these steps every year on March 15.

The museum's most sacred treasure, the **Szent Korona** (Holy Crown), reposes with other royal relics in a domed Hall of Honor off the main lobby. The crown sits like a golden soufflé above a Byzantine band of holy scenes in enamel and pearls and other gems. It seems to date from the 12th century, so it could not be the crown that Pope Sylvester II presented to St. Stephen in the year 1000, when he was crowned the first king of Hungary. Nevertheless, it is known as the Crown of St. Stephen and has been regarded—even by Communist governments—as the legal symbol of Hungarian sovereignty and unbroken statehood. In 1945 the fleeing Hungarian army handed over the crown and its accompanying regalia to the Americans rather than have them fall into Soviet hands. They were restored to Hungary in 1978.

Other rarities include a completely furnished Turkish tent; masterworks of cabinet making and wood carving, including pews from churches in Nyírbátor and Transylvania; a piano that belonged to both Beethoven and Liszt; and, in the treasury, masterpieces of goldsmithing, among them the 11th-century Constantions Monomachos crown from Byzantium and the richly pictorial 16th-century chalice of Miklós Pálffy. Looking at it is like reading the "Prince Valiant" comic strip in gold. The epic Hungarian history exhibit has exhibits chronicling the end of communism and the much-celebrated exodus of the Russian troops. ⊠ *IX, Múzeum körút 14–16,* ☎ *1/338–2122.* ▣ *270 Ft.* ☉ *Mid-Mar.–mid-Oct., Wed.–Sun. 10–6; mid-Oct.–mid-Mar., Wed.–Sun. 10–5. Museum may open Tues. also, depending on demand; call ahead to check.*

★ ㊷ **Nagy Zsinagóga** (Great Synagogue). Seating 3,000, Europe's largest synagogue was designed by Ludwig Förs and built between 1844 and 1859 in a Byzantine-Moorish style described as "consciously archaic Romantic-Eastern." Desecrated by German and Hungarian Nazis, it was painstakingly reconstructed with donations from all over the world; its doors reopened in fall 1996. While it is used for regular services during much of the year, it is generally not used in midwinter as the space is too large to heat; between December and February, visiting hours are erratic. In the courtyard behind the synagogue, a weeping willow made of metal honors the victims of the Holocaust. Liszt and Saint-Saëns are among the great musicians who have played its grand organ. ⊠ *Dohány u. 2–8,* ☎ *1/342–1335.* ▣ *Free.* ☉ *Weekdays 10–3, Sun. 10–1. Closed Jewish holidays and Dec.*

★ ㉙ **Néprajzi Múzeum** (Museum of Ethnography). The 1890s neoclassical temple formerly housed the Supreme Court. Now an impressive permanent exhibition, "The Folk Culture of the Hungarian People," explains all aspects of peasant life from the end of the 18th century until World War I; explanatory texts are provided in both English and Hungarian. Besides embroideries, pottery, and carvings—the authentic pieces you can't see at touristy folk shops—there are farming tools, furniture, and traditional costumes. The central room of the building alone is worth the entrance fee: a majestic hall with ornate marble staircases and pillars, and towering stained-glass windows. ✉ *V, Kossuth tér 12,* ☎ *1/332–6340.* ✆ *250 Ft., Tues. free.* ☉ *Mid-Mar.–mid-Oct., Tues.–Sun. 10–6; mid-Oct.–mid-Mar., Tues.–Sun. 10–4.*

★ **㉘ Országház** (Parliament). The most visible, though not highly accessible, symbol of Budapest's left bank is the huge neo-Gothic Parliament. Mirrored in the Danube much the way Britain's Parliament is reflected by the Thames, it lies midway between the Margaret and Chain bridges and can be reached by the M2 subway (Kossuth tér station) and waterfront Tram 2. A fine example of historicizing, eclectic fin-de-siècle architecture, it was designed by the Hungarian architect Ímre Steindl and built by a thousand workers between 1885 and 1902. The grace and dignity of its long facade and 24 slender towers, with spacious arcades and high windows balancing its vast central dome, lend this living landmark a refreshingly Baroque spatial effect. The exterior is lined with 90 statues of great figures in Hungarian history; the corbels are ornamented by 242 allegorical statues. Inside are 691 rooms, 10 courtyards, and 29 staircases; some 88 pounds of gold were used for the staircases and halls. These halls are also a gallery of late-19th-century Hungarian art, with frescoes and canvases depicting Hungarian history, starting with Mihály Munkácsy's large painting of the Magyar Conquest of 896. Unfortunately, because Parliament is a workplace for legislators, the building is not open to individual visitors and must be toured in groups at certain hours on specific city tours organized by IBUSZ Travel (☞ Sightseeing Tours *in* Essential Information). ✉ *V, Kossuth tér.*

✓ **㉛ Roosevelt tér** (Roosevelt Square). This square opening onto the Danube is less closely connected with the U.S. president than with the progressive Hungarian statesman Count István Széchenyi, dubbed "the greatest Hungarian" even by his adversary, Kossuth. The neo-Renaissance palace of the **Magyar Tudományos Akadémia** (Academy of Sciences) on the north side was built between 1862 and 1864, after Széchenyi's suicide. It is a fitting memorial, for in 1825, the statesman donated a year's income from all his estates to establish the academy. Another Széchenyi project, the

Széchenyi Lánchíd (☞ *below*), leads into the square; there stands a statue of Széchenyi near one of another statesman, Ferenc Deák, whose negotiations led to the establishment of the dual monarchy after Kossuth's 1848–1849 revolution failed. Both men lived on this square.

★ ㉚ **Szabadság tér** (Liberty Square). This is the site of the **Magyar Televizió** (Hungarian Television Headquarters), a former stock exchange with what look like four temples and two castles on its roof, and a solemn-looking neoclassical shrine, the **Nemzeti Bank** (National Bank). The bank's Postal Savings Bank branch, adjacent to the main building but visible from behind Szabadság tér on Hold utca, is another exuberant Art Nouveau masterpiece of architect Ödön Lechner, built in 1901 with colorful majolica mosaics, characteristically curvaceous windows, and pointed towers ending in swirling gold flourishes. In the square's center remains one of the few monuments to the Russian "liberation" that were spared the recent cleansing of symbols of the past regime. The decision to retain this obelisk—because it represents liberation from the Nazis during World War II—caused outrage among many groups, prompting some to vow to haul it away themselves (though for the moment it remains). With the Stars and Stripes flying out in front, the **American Embassy** is at Szabadság tér 12.

Széchenyi Lánchíd (Chain Bridge). This is the oldest and most beautiful of the Danube's eight bridges. Before it was built, the river could be crossed only by ferry or by a pontoon bridge that had to be removed when ice blocks began floating downstream in winter. It was constructed at the initiative of the great Hungarian reformer and philanthropist Count István Széchenyi, using an 1839 design by the French civil engineer William Tierney Clark. This classical, almost poetically graceful and symmetrical suspension bridge was finished by his Scottish namesake, Adam Clark, who also built the 383-yard tunnel under Castle Hill, thus connecting the Danube quay with the rest of Buda. After it was destroyed by the Nazis, the bridge was rebuilt in its original form (though slightly widened for traffic) and was reopened in 1949, on the centenary of its inauguration. At the Buda end of the bridge is **Clark Ádám tér** (Adam Clark Square), where you can zip up to Castle Hill on the sometimes crowded Sikló funicular rail. 🖃 *250 Ft.* ⊙ *Funicular daily 7:30 AM–10 PM; closed every other Mon.*

★ ㊺ **Szent István Bazilika** (St. Stephen's Basilica). Dark and massive, this is one of the chief landmarks of Pest and the city's largest church—it can hold 8,500 people. Its very Holy Roman front porch greets you with a tympanum bustling with statuary. The basilica's dome and the dome of Parliament are by far the most visible in the Pest skyline, and this is no accident: With the Magyar Millennium of 1896 in mind, both domes were planned to be 315 ft high.

The millennium was not yet in sight when architect József Hild began building the basilica in neoclassical style in 1851, two years after the revolution was suppressed. After Hild's death, the project was taken over in 1867 by Miklós Ybl, the architect who did the most to transform modern Pest into a monumental metropolis. Wherever he could, Ybl shifted Hild's motifs toward the neo-Renaissance mode that Ybl favored. When the dome collapsed, partly damaging the walls, he made even more drastic changes. Ybl died in 1891, five years before the 1,000-year celebration, and the basilica was completed in neo-Renaissance style by József Kauser—but not until 1905.

Below the cupola is a rich collection of late-19th-century Hungarian art: mosaics, altarpieces, and statuary (what heady days the millennium must have meant for local talents!). There are 150 kinds of marble, all from Hungary except for the Carrara in the sanctuary's centerpiece: a white statue of King (St.) Stephen I, Hungary's first king and patron saint. Stephen's mummified right hand is preserved as a relic in the **Szent Jobb Kápolna** (Holy Right Chapel); the guard will illuminate it for you for two minutes for a minimal charge. Visitors can also climb the 364 stairs (or take the elevator) to the top of the cupola for a spectacular view of the city. Extensive restorations have been under way at the aging basilica for years, with a target completion date of 2010, and some part of the structure is likely to be under scaffolding when you visit. ⊠ *V, Szt. István tér,* ☎ *1/317–2859.* 🖃 *Church free, Szt. Jobb chapel 100 Ft., cupola 350 Ft.* ⊙ *Church Mon.–Sat. 7–7, Sun. 1–7; Szt. Jobb Chapel Apr.–Sept., Mon.–Sat. 9–5, Sun. 1–5; Oct.–*

Mar., Mon.–Sat. 10–4, Sun. 1–4; Cupola Apr. and Sept.–Oct., daily 10–5; May–Aug., daily 9–6.

Szerb Ortodox templom (Serbian Orthodox Church). Built in 1688, this lovely burnt-orange church, one of Budapest's oldest buildings, sits in a shaded garden surrounded by thick stone walls of the same color detailed with large-tile mosaics and wrought-iron gates. ⊠ *V, Szerb utca.*

❸❻ Váci utca. Immediately north of Elizabeth Bridge is Budapest's best-known shopping street and most unabashed tourist zone, Váci utca, a pedestrian precinct with electrified 19th-century lampposts and smart shops with credit-card emblems on ornate doorways. No bargain basement, Váci utca gets its special flavor from the mix of native furriers, tailors, designers, shoemakers, and folk artists, as well as an increasing number of internationally known boutiques. There are also bookstores and china and crystal shops, as well as gourmet food stores redolent of paprika. Váci utca's second half, south of Kossuth Lajos utca, was transformed into another pedestrian-only zone a few years ago and has a different character from its northern side. The street is a clash of past and future: A tiny button shop and a knife and scissor sharpening store struggle alongside tacky souvenir vendors and flashy boutiques. Watch your purses and wallets—against inflated prices *and* active pickpockets.

❹❸ Városház. The monumental former city council building, which used to be a hospital for wounded soldiers and then a resort for the elderly ("home" would be too cozy for so vast a hulk), is now Budapest's city hall. It's enormous enough to loom over the row of shops and businesses lining Károly körút in front of it but can only be entered through courtyards or side streets (Gerlóczy utca is the most accessible). The Tuscan columns at the main entrance and the allegorical statuary of *Atlas, War,* and *Peace* are especially splendid. There was once a chapel in the center of the main facade, but now only its spire remains. ⊠ *V, Városház u. 9–12,* ☎ *1/318–6066.*

❸❾ Vásárcsarnok (Central Market Hall). The magnificent hall, a 19th-century iron-frame construction, was reopened in late 1994 after years of renovation (and disputes over who would foot the bill). Even during the leanest years of Communist shortages, the abundance of food came as a revelation to shoppers from East and West. Today, the cavernous, three-story hall once again teems with people browsing among stalls packed with salamis and red-paprika chains. Upstairs you can buy folk embroideries and souvenirs. ⊠ *IX, Vámhaz körút 1–3.* ⊙ *Mon. 6 AM–5 PM, Tues.–Fri. 6 AM–6 PM, Sat. 6 AM–2 PM.*

③③ **Vigadó** (Concert Hall). Designed in a striking romantic style by Frigyes Feszl and inaugurated in 1865 with Franz Liszt conducting his own *St. Elizabeth Oratorio,* the concert hall is a curious mixture of Byzantine, Moorish, Romanesque, and Hungarian motifs, punctuated by dancing statues and sturdy pillars. Brahms, Debussy, and Casals are among the other phenomenal musicians who have graced its stage. Mahler's *Symphony No. 1* and many works by Bartók were first performed here. While you can go into the lobby on your own, the hall is open only for concerts. ⊠ *V, Vigadó tér 2.*

★ **③⑤** **Vörösmarty tér** (Vörösmarty Square). This large, handsome square at the northern end of Váci utca is the heart of Pest's tourist life. Street musicians and sidewalk cafés make it one of the liveliest places in Budapest and a good spot to sit and relax—if you can ward off the aggressive caricature sketchers. Grouped around a white-marble statue of the 19th-century poet and dramatist Mihály Vörösmarty are luxury shops, airline offices, and an elegant former pissoir. Now a lovely kiosk, it displays gold-painted historic scenes of the square's golden days.

Zsidó Múzeum (Jewish Museum). The four-room museum, around the corner from the Great Synagogue (☞ *above*), has displays explaining the effect of the Holocaust on Hungarian and Transylvanian Jews, as well as those highlighting the rituals and traditions of Hungary's Jewish culture. (There are labels in English.) In late 1993, burglars ransacked the museum and got away with approximately 80% of its priceless collection; several months later, the stolen objects were found in Romania and returned to their home. ⊠ *Dohány utca 2,* ☎ *1/342–8949.* ⌑ *150 Ft. suggested donation.* ⊙ *Mon.–Thurs. 10–6, Fri. 10–3, Sun. 10–2.*

Andrássy út

Behind St. Stephen's Basilica, at the crossroad along Bajcsy-Zsilinszky út, begins Budapest's grandest avenue, **Andrássy út.** For too many years, this broad boulevard bore the tongue-twisting name of Népköztársaság útja (Avenue of the People's Republic) and, for a while before that, Stalin Avenue. In 1990, however, it reverted to its old name honoring Count Gyula Andrássy, a statesman who in 1867 became the first constitutional premier of Hungary. The boulevard that would eventually bear his name was begun in 1872, as Buda and Pest (and Óbuda) were about to be unified. Most of the mansions that line it were completed by 1884. It took another dozen years before the first **underground railway** on the Continent was completed for—you guessed it—the Magyar Millennium in 1896. Though preceded by London's Underground (1863), Budapest's was the world's first electrified subway. Only slightly modernized but refurbished for the 1996 millecentenary, this "Little Metro" is still running a 4-km (2½-mi) stretch from Vörösmarty tér to the far end of City Park. Using tiny yellow trains with tanklike treads, and stopping at antique stations marked FÖLDALATTI (Underground) on their wrought-iron entranceways, Line 1 is a tourist attraction in itself. Six of its 10 stations are along Andrássy út.

A GOOD WALK

A walking tour of Andrássy út's sights is straightforward: Begin at its downtown end, near Deák tér, and stroll its length (about 2 km/1¼ mi) all the way to **Hősök tere** ㊿. The first third of the avenue, from Bajcsy-Zsilinszky út to the eight-sided intersection called Oktogon, boasts a row of eclectic city palaces with balconies held up by stone giants. Pause at the **Operaház** ㊼ and other points along the way. One block past the Operaház, Andrássy út intersects Budapest's Broadway: Nagymező utca contains several theaters, cabarets, and nightclubs. Andrássy út alters when it crosses the Nagy körút (Outer Ring Road), at the Oktogon crossing. Four rows of trees and scores of flower beds make the thoroughfare look more like a garden promenade, but its cultural character lingers. Farther up, past **Kodály körönd,** the rest of Andrássy út is dominated by widely spaced mansions surrounded by private gardens. At Hősök tere, browse through the **Mücsarnok** ㊾ and/or the **Szépmű-vészeti Múzeum** ㊿, and finish off with a stroll into the Városliget (City Park; ☞ *below*). You can return to Deák tér on the subway, the Millenniumi Földalatti (Millennial Underground).

TIMING

As most museums are closed Mondays, it's best to explore Andrássy út on other days, preferably weekdays or early Saturday, when stores are also open for browsing. During opera season, you can time your exploration to land you at the Operaház stairs just before 7 PM to watch the spectacle of opera goers flowing in for the evening's performance.

SIGHTS TO SEE

⟲ **Budapest Bábszínház** (Budapest Puppet Theater). In this templelike, eclectic building, you'll find colorful shows that both children and adults deem enjoyable even if they don't understand Hungarian. Watch for showings of *Cinderella* (*Hamupipőke*) and *Snow White and the Seven Dwarfs* (*Hófehérke*), part of the theater's regular repertoire. ⊠ *VI, Andrássy út 69*, ☎ *1/322–5200*.

Drechsler Kastély (Drechsler Palace). Across the street from the Operaház is the French Renaissance–style Drechsler Palace. An early work by Ödön Lechner, Hungary's master of Art Nouveau, it is now the home of the National Ballet School. ⊠ *VI, Andrássy út 25*.

Hopp Ferenc Kelet-Ázsiai Művészeti Múzeum (Ferenc Hopp Museum of Eastern Asiatic Arts). Stop in here to see the rich collection of exotica from the Indian subcontinent, such as sculpture and devotional pieces, and Far Eastern ceramics. ⊠ *Andrássy út 103*, ☎ *1/322–8476*. ⌦ *80 Ft.* ☉ *Oct.–mid-Apr., Tues.–Sun. 10–4; mid-Apr.–Sept., Tues.–Sun. 10–6*.

★ ㉛ **Hősök tere** (Heroes' Square). Andrássy út ends in grandeur at Heroes' Square, with Budapest's answer to Berlin's Brandenburg Gate. Cleaned and refurbished in 1996 for the millecentenary, the **Millenniumi Emlékmű** (Millennial Monument) is a semicircular twin colonnade with statues of Hungary's kings and leaders between its pillars. Set back in its open center, a 118-ft stone column is crowned by a dynamic statue of the archangel Gabriel, his outstretched arms bearing the ancient emblems of Hungary. At its base ride seven bronze horsemen: the Magyar chieftains, led by Árpád, whose tribes conquered the land in 896. Before the column lies a simple marble slab, the **Nemzeti Háborús Emlék Tábla** (National War Memorial), the nation's altar, at which every visiting foreign dignitary lays a ceremonial wreath. England's Queen Elizabeth upheld the tradition during her royal visit in May of 1992. In 1991 Pope John Paul II conducted a mass here. Just a few months earlier, half a million Hungarians had convened to recall the memory of Imre Nagy, the reform-minded Communist prime minister who partially inspired the 1956 revolution. Heroes' Square is flanked by the **Műcsarnok** and the **Szépművészeti Múzeum** (☞ *below*).

Kodály körönd. A handsome traffic circle with imposing statues of three Hungarian warriors—leavened by a fourth one of a poet—the Kodály körönd is surrounded by plane and chestnut trees. Look carefully at the towered mansions on the north side of the circle—behind the soot you'll see the fading colors of ornate frescoes peeking through. The circle takes its name from the composer Zoltán Kodály, who lived just beyond it at Andrássy út 89.

50 **Liszt Ferenc Emlékmúzeum** (Franz Liszt Memorial Museum). Andrássy út No. 67 was the original location of the old Academy of Music and Franz Liszt's last home; entered around the corner, it now houses a museum. Several rooms display the original furniture and instruments from Liszt's time there; another room shows temporary exhibits. The museum hosts excellent, free classical concerts year round, except in August. ⊠ *Vörösmarty u. 35,* ☎ *1/342–7320.* ☜ *100 Ft.* ☉ *Weekdays 10–6, Sat. 9–5. Classical concerts (free with admission) Sept.–July, Sat. 11 AM. Closed Aug. 1–20.*

49 **Liszt Ferenc Zeneakadémia** (Franz Liszt Academy of Music). Along with the **Vigadó** (☞ Downtown Pest and the Kis körút, *above*), this is one of the city's main concert halls. The academy in fact has two auditoriums: a green-and-gold 1,200-seat main hall and a smaller hall for chamber music and solo recitals. Outside this exuberant Art Nouveau building, a statue of Liszt oversees the square. The academy has been operating as a highly revered teaching institute since

1907; Liszt was its first chairman and Erkel its first director. The pianist Ernő (formerly Ernst) Dohnányi and com-
posers Béla Bartók and Zoltán Kodály were teachers here.
⊠ *Liszt Ferenc tér 8,* ☏ *1/342–0179.*

㊽ Mai Manó Fotógaléria (Mai Manó Photo Gallery). This
weathered yet ornate turn-of-the-century building was
built as a photography studio, where the wealthy bour-
geoisie would come to be photographed by imperial and
royal court photographer Manó Mai. Inside, ironwork and
frescoes ornament the curving staircase leading up to the
tiny gallery, the only one in Budapest that is exclusively
devoted to photography. Restorations are under way to re-
juvenate the tired old building and to expand the facilities. ⊠ *V, Nagymező u. 20,* ☏ *1/302–4398.* ▨ *Free.* ☉
Weekdays 2–6.

㊾ Műcsarnok (Palace of Exhibitions). The city's largest hall
for special exhibitions is a striking 1895 temple of culture
with a colorful tympanum. After four years of exhaustive
renovations, the Palace of Exhibitions reopened its doors
during the 1995 Budapest Spring Festival. Its program of
events includes exhibitions of contemporary Hungarian
and international art and a rich series of films, plays, and
concerts. ⊠ *XIV, Dózsa György út 37,* ☏ *1/343–7401.* ▨
250 Ft., Tues. free. ☉ *Tues.–Sun. 10–6.*

★ ㊼ Operaház (Opera House). Miklós Ybl's crowning achieve-
ment is the neo-Renaissance Opera House, built between
1875 and 1884. Badly damaged during the siege of 1944–
1945, it was restored for its 1984 centenary. Two buxom
marble sphinxes guard the driveway; the main entrance is
flanked by Alajos Strobl's "romantic-realist" limestone
statues of Liszt and of another 19th-century Hungarian composer, Ferenc Erkel, the father of Hungarian opera (his pa-
triotic opera *Bánk bán* is still performed for national
celebrations).

Inside, the spectacle begins even before the performance does.
You glide up grand staircases and through wood-paneled
corridors and gilt lime-green salons into a glittering jewel
box of an auditorium. Its four tiers of boxes are held up by
helmeted sphinxes beneath a frescoed ceiling by Károly
Lotz. Lower down there are frescoes everywhere, with in-

tertwined motifs of Apollo and Dionysus. In its early years, the Budapest Opera was conducted by Gustav Mahler (from 1888 to 1891) and, after World War II, by Otto Klemperer.

The best way to experience the Opera House's interior is to see a ballet or opera; and while performance quality varies, tickets are relatively cheap and easy to come by, at least by tourist standards. And descending from *La Bohème* into the Földalatti station beneath the Opera House was described by travel writer Stephen Brook in *The Double Eagle* as stepping "out of one period piece and into another." There are no performances in summer, except for the weeklong BudaFest international opera and ballet festival in mid-August. Fifty-minute tours (in English) are usually conducted daily at 3 PM and 4 PM; meet by the sphinx at the Dálszínház utca entrance. (Call ahead to confirm that one is being given). The cost is about 900 Ft. ⊠ *VI, Andrássy út 22,* ☎ *1/331–2550 (ext. 156 for tours).*

㊻ Postamúzeum (Postal Museum). The best of Andrássy út's many marvelous stone mansions is luckily visitable, for the Postal Museum occupies an apartment with frescoes by Károly Lotz (whose work adorns St. Stephen's Basilica and the Opera House). Among the displays is an exhibition on the history of Hungarian mail, radio, and telecommunications. There are English-language pamphlets available. Even if the exhibits don't thrill you, the venue is worth the visit. ⊠ *Andrássy út 3,* ☎ *1/269–6838.* 🎫 *70 Ft.* ☉ *Tues.– Sun. 10–6.*

★ ㊾ Szépművészeti Múzeum (Museum of Fine Arts). Across Heroes' Square from the Palace of Exhibitions and built by the same team of Albert Schickedanz and Fülöp Herzog, the Museum of Fine Arts houses Hungary's finest collection, rich in Flemish and Dutch old masters. With seven fine El Grecos and five beautiful Goyas as well as paintings by Velázquez and Murillo, the collection of Spanish old masters is one of the best outside Spain. The Italian school is represented by Giorgione, Bellini, Correggio, Tintoretto, and Titian masterpieces and, above all, two superb Raphael paintings: *Eszterházy Madonna* and his immortal *Portrait of a Youth,* rescued after a world-famous art heist. Nineteenth-century French art includes works by Delacroix, Pissarro, Cézanne, Toulouse-Lautrec, Gauguin, Renoir, and Monet.

There are also more than 100,000 drawings (including five by Rembrandt and three studies by Leonardo), Egyptian and Greco-Roman exhibitions, late-Gothic winged altars from northern Hungary and Transylvania, and works by all the leading figures of Hungarian art up to the present. A 20th-century collection was added to the museum's permanent exhibits in 1994, comprising an interesting series of statues, paintings, and drawings by Chagall, Le Corbusier, and others. Labels are in both Hungarian and English; there's also an English-language booklet on the permanent collection for sale. ⊠ XIV, Dózsa György út 41, ☎ 1/343–9759. ☞ 250 Ft. ☉ Tues.–Sun. 10–5:30.

Városliget (City Park)

A GOOD WALK

Heroes' Square is the gateway to the **Városliget** (City Park): a square km (almost half a square mi) of recreation, entertainment, beauty, and culture. A bridge behind the Millennial Monument leads across a boating basin that becomes an artificial ice-skating rink in winter; to the south of this lake stands a statue of George Washington, erected in 1906 with donations by Hungarian emigrants to the United States. Next to the lake stands **Vajdahunyad Vár,** built in myriad architectural styles. Visitors can soak or swim at the turn-of-the-century Széchenyi Fürdő, jog along the park paths, or careen on Vidám Park's roller coaster. There's also the Petőfi Csarnok, a leisure-time youth center and major concert hall on the site of an old industrial exhibition.

TIMING

Fair-weather weekends, when the children's attractions are teeming with kids and parents and the Széchenyi Fürdő brimming with bathers, are the best time for people-watchers to visit City Park; if you go on a weekday, the main sights are rarely crowded.

SIGHTS TO SEE

☾ **Budapesti Állatkert** (Budapest Zoo). This fairly depressing urban zoo is brightened—for humans, anyway—by an elephant pavilion decorated with Zsolnay majolica and glazed ceramic animals. ⊠ XIV, Állatkerti körút 6–12, ☎ 1/343–6073. ☞ 400 Ft. ☉ Mar. and Oct., daily 9–5; Apr. and Sept., *daily 9–6; May, daily 9–6:30; June–Aug., daily 9–7; Nov.–Feb., daily 9–4 (last tickets sold 1 hr before closing).*

♻ **Fővárosi Nagycirkusz** (Municipal Grand Circus). This circus puts on colorful performances by local acrobats, clowns, and animal trainers, as well as by international guests, in its small ring. The performance schedule varies from November to June; you'll need to call ahead. ⊠ *XIV, Állatkerti körút 7,* ☎ *1/343–8300.* 🎟 *Weekdays 350–650 Ft., weekends 400–750 Ft.* ☼ *July–Aug., Wed.–Sat. 3 PM and 7 PM, Sun. 10 AM and 3 PM; closed Sept.–Oct.*

Széchenyi Fürdő (Széchenyi Baths). Dating from 1876, these vast baths are in a beautiful neo-Baroque building in the middle of City Park; they comprise one of the biggest spas in Europe. There are several thermal pools indoors as well as two outdoors, which remain open even in winter, when dense steam hangs thick over the hot water's surface—you can just barely make out the figures of elderly men, submerged shoulder deep, crowded around waterproof chessboards. ⊠ *XIV, Állatkerti körút 11,* ☎ *1/321–0310.* 🎟 *450 Ft.* ☼ *May–Sept., daily 6–6; Oct.–Apr., daily 6–5.*

★ **Vajdahunyad Vár** (Vajdahunyad Castle). Beside the City Park's lake stands this castle, an art historian's Disneyland. The fantastic medley borrows from all of Hungary's historic and architectural past, starting with the Romanesque gateway of the cloister of Jak in western Hungary. A Gothic castle, Transylvanian turrets, Renaissance loggia, Baroque portico, and Byzantine decoration are all guarded by a spooky modern (1903) bronze statue of the anonymous medieval chronicler who was the first recorder of Hungarian history. Designed for the millennial celebration in 1896 but not completed until 1908, this hodgepodge houses the surprisingly interesting **Mezőgazdasági Múzeum** (Agricultural Museum), with intriguingly arranged sections on animal husbandry, forestry, horticulture, hunting, and fishing. ⊠ *XIV, Városliget, Széchenyi Island,* ☎ *1/343–3198.* 🎟 *Museum 170 Ft.* ☼ *Mid-Feb.–Nov., Tues.–Sat. 10–5, Sun. 10–6; Dec.–mid-Feb., Tues.–Fri. 10–4, weekends 10–5.*

♻ **Vidám Park.** Budapest's somewhat weary amusement park is next to the zoo and is crawling with happy children with their parents or grandparents in tow. Rides cost around $1 (some are for preschoolers). There are also game rooms and a scenic railway. Next to the main park is a separate, smaller section for toddlers. In winter, only a few rides operate. ⊠ *Városliget, Állatkerti krt. 14–16,* ☎ *1/343–0996.* 🎫 *100 Ft.* ⊗ *Mid-Mar.–Aug., daily 10–7; Sept.–mid-Mar., daily 10–late afternoon.*

Eastern Pest and the Nagy körút (Great Ring Road)

This section covers primarily Kossuth Lajos–Rákóczi út and the Nagykörút (Great Ring Road)—busy, less-touristy urban thoroughfares full of people, cars, shops, and Budapest's unique urban flavor.

Beginning a few blocks from the Elizabeth Bridge, Kossuth Lajos utca is Budapest's busiest shopping street. Try to look above and beyond the store windows to the architecture and activity along Kossuth Lajos utca and its continuation, Rákóczi út, which begins when it crosses the Kis körút (Little Ring Road) at the busy intersection called Astoria. Most of Rákóczi út is lined with hotels, shops, and department stores and it ends at the grandiose Keleti (Eastern) Railway Station.

Pest's Great Ring Road, the Nagy körút, was laid out at the end of the 19th century in a wide semicircle anchored to the Danube at both ends; an arm of the river was covered over to create this 114-ft-wide thoroughfare. The large apartment buildings on both sides also date from this era. Along with theaters, stores, and cafés, they form a boulevard unique in Europe for its "unified eclecticism," which blends a variety of historic styles into a harmonious whole. Its entire length of almost 4½ km (2¾ mi) from Margaret Bridge to Petőfi Bridge is traversed by Trams 4 and 6, but strolling it in stretches is also a good way to experience the hustle and bustle of downtown Budapest.

Like its smaller counterpart, the Kis körút (Little Ring Road), the Great Ring Road comprises sectors of various names. Beginning with Ferenc körút at the Petőfi Bridge, it changes to József körút at the intersection marked by the Museum of Applied Arts, then to Erzsébet körút at Blaha Lujza Square. Teréz körút begins at the busy Oktogon crossing with Andrássy út and ends at the Nyugati (West) Railway Station, where Szent István takes over for the final stretch to the Margaret Bridge.

A GOOD WALK

Beginning with a visit to the **Iparművészeti Múzeum** 54, near the southern end of the boulevard, walk or take Tram 4 or 6 north (away from the Petőfi Bridge) to the New York Kávéház on Erzsébet körút, just past Blaha Lujza tér—all in all about 1¾ km (1 mi) from the museum. The neo-Rennaissance **Keleti pályaudvar** is a one-metro-stop detour away from Blaha Lujza tér. Continuing in the same direction on the körút, go several stops on the tram to **Nyugati pályaudvar** and walk the remaining sector, Szent István körút, past the **Vígszínház** 57 to Margaret Bridge. From the bridge, views of Margaret Island, to the north, and Parliament, Castle Hill, the Chain Bridge, and Gellért Hill, to the south, are gorgeous.

TIMING

As this area is packed with stores, it's best to explore during store hours—weekdays until around 5 PM and Saturdays until 1 PM; Saturdays will be most crowded. Keep in mind that the Iparművészeti Múzeum is closed Mondays.

SIGHTS TO SEE

★ 54 **Iparművészeti Múzeum** (Museum of Applied and Decorative Arts). The templelike structure housing this museum is indeed a shrine to Hungarian Art Nouveau, and in front of it, drawing pen in hand, sits a statue of its creator, Hungarian architect Ödön Lechner. Opened in the millennial year of 1896, it was only the third museum of its kind in Europe. Its dome of tiles is crowned by a majolica lantern from the same source: the Zsolnay ceramic works in Pécs. Inside its central hall are playfully swirling whitewashed, double-decker, Moorish-style galleries and arcades. The museum, which collects and studies objects of interior decoration and use, has five departments: furniture, textiles, goldsmithing, ceramics, and everyday objects. ⊠ *Üllői út 33–37,* ☎ *1/217–5222.* 🎟 *170 Ft.* ☉ *Tues.–Sun. 10–6.*

55 **Kapel Szent Roch** (St. Roch Chapel). The impact of this charming, yellow, 18th-century chapel is rendered even more colorful by peasant women peddling lace and em-

broidery on its small square. The chapel is the oldest remnant of Pest's former outer district. It was built beside a hospice where doomed victims of the great plague of 1711 were sent to die as far away as possible from residential areas. ⊠ *Corner of Rákóczi út and Gyulai Pál utca.*

Keleti pályaudvar (Eastern Railway Station). The grandiose, imperial-looking Eastern Railway Station was built in 1884 and considered Europe's most modern until well into this century. Its neo-Renaissance facade, which resembles a gateway, is flanked by statues of two British inventors and railway pioneers, James Watt and George Stephenson. ⊠ *VII, Rákóczi út.*

⑤⑥ **Köztársaság tér** (Square of the Republic). Surrounded by faceless concrete buildings, this square is not particularly alluring aesthetically but is significant because it was where the Communist Party of Budapest had its headquarters, and it was also the scene of heavy fighting in 1956. Here also is the city's second opera house, and Budapest's largest, the **Erkel Ferenc színház** (Ferenc Erkel Theatre).

Nyugati pályaudvar (Western Railway Station). The iron-laced glass hall of the Western Railway Station is in complete contrast to—and much more modern than—the newer Eastern Railway Station. Built in the 1870s, it was designed by a team of architects from Gustav Eiffel's office in Paris. ⊠ *VI, Teréz krt.*

Párizsi Udvar (Paris Court). This glass-roofed arcade was built in 1914 in richly ornamental neo-Gothic and eclectic styles—it's one of the most attractive sights of Pest. Nowadays it's filled with touristy boutiques. ⊠ *Corner of Petőfi Sándor utca and Kossuth Lajos utca.*

★ ⑤⑦ **Vígszínház** (Comedy Theater). This neo-Baroque, late-19th-century, gemlike theater twinkles with just a tiny, playful anticipation of Art Nouveau and sparkles inside and out since its 1994 refurbishment. The theater hosts primarily musicals, such as Hungarian adaptations of *Cats,* as well as dance performances and classical concerts. ⊠ *XIII, Pannónia u. 1,* ☎ *1/329–2340.*

Óbuda

Until its unification with Buda and Pest in 1872 to form the city of Budapest, Óbuda (the name means Old Buda) was a separate town that used to be the main settlement; now it is usually thought of as a suburb. Although the vast new apartment blocks of Budapest's biggest housing project and busy roadways are what first strike the eye, the historic core of Óbuda has been preserved in its entirety.

A GOOD WALK

Óbuda is easily reached by car, bus, or streetcar via the Árpád Bridge from Pest or by the HÉV suburban railway from Batthyány tér to the Árpád Bridge. Once you're there, covering all the sights on foot involves large but manageable distances along major exhaust-permeated roadways. One way to tackle it is to take Tram 17 from its southern terminus at the Buda side of the Margaret Bridge to Kiscelli utca and walk uphill to the **Kiscelli Múzeum.** Then walk back down the same street all the way past **Flórián tér,** continuing toward the Danube and making a left onto Hídfő utca or Szentlélek tér to enter **Fő tér.** After exploring the square and taking in the museums in the **Zichy Kúria,** walk a block or two southeast to the HÉV suburban railway stop and take the train just north to the museum complex at **Aquincum.**

TIMING

It's best to begin touring Óbuda during the cooler, early hours of the day, as the heat on the area's busy roads can get overbearing. Avoid Mondays, when museums are closed.

SIGHTS TO SEE

Aquincum. This complex comprises the reconstructed remains of a Roman settlement dating from the 1st century AD and the capital of the Roman province of Pannonia. Careful excavations have unearthed a varied selection of artifacts and mosaics, giving a tantalizing inkling of what life was like in the provinces of the Roman Empire. A gymnasium and a central heating system have been unearthed, along with the ruins of two baths and a shrine to Mithras, the Persian god of light, truth, and the sun. The **Aquincum múzeum** (Aquincum Museum) displays the dig's most notable finds: ceramics; a red-marble sarcophagus showing a triton and flying Eros on one side and on the other, Telesphorus, the angel of death, depicted as a hooded dwarf; and jewelry from a Roman lady's tomb. ⊠ *III, Szentendrei út 139,* ☎ *1/250–1650.* 🖅 *350 Ft.* ☉ *Mid-Apr.–end of Apr. and Oct., Tues.–Sun. 10–5; May–Sept., Tues.–Sun. 10–6. Grounds open at 9.*

Flórián tér. The center of today's Óbuda is Flórián tér, where Roman ruins were first discovered when the foundations of a house were dug in 1778. Two centuries later, careful excavations were carried out during the reconstruction of the square, and today the restored ancient ruins lie in the center of the square in boggling contrast to the racing traffic and cement-block housing projects.

Fő tér. Óbuda's charming old main square is its most picturesque part. The square has been spruced up in recent years, and there are now several good restaurants and interesting museums in and around the Baroque **Zichy Kúria** (☞ *below*), which has become a neighborhood cultural center. Among the most popular offerings are the summer concerts in the courtyard and the evening jazz concerts.

Hercules Villa. A fine 3rd-century Roman dwelling, it takes its name from the myth depicted on its beautiful mosaic floor. The ruin was unearthed between 1958 and 1967 and is now only open by request (inquire at Aquincum). ⊠ *III, Meggyfa u. 19–21.*

Kiscelli Múzeum (Kiscelli Museum). A strenuous climb up the steep, dilapidated sidewalks of Remethegy (Hermit's Hill) will deposit you at this elegant, mustard-yellow Baroque mansion. Built between 1744 and 1760 as a Trinitarian monastery, today it holds an eclectic mix of paintings, sculptures, engravings, and sundry items related to the history of Budapest. Included here is the printing press on which poet and revolutionary Sándor Petőfi printed his famous "Nemzeti Dal" ("National Song") in 1848, inciting the Hungarian people to rise up against the Hapsburgs. ⊠ *III, Kiscelli u. 108,* ☎ *1/250–0304.* 🖅 *170 Ft.* ☉ *Nov.–Mar., Tues.–Sun. 10–4; Apr.–Oct., Tues.–Sun. 10–6.*

Római amfiteátrum (Roman Amphitheater). Probably dating back to the 2nd century, Óbuda's Roman military amphitheater once held some 16,000 people and, at 144 yards in diameter, was one of Europe's largest. A block of dwellings

called the Round House was later built by the Romans above
the amphitheater; massive stone walls found in the Round
House's cellar were actually parts of the amphitheater.
Below the amphitheater are the cells where prisoners and
lions were held while awaiting confrontation. It's open to
the public, more by nonchalance than design—people sometimes use it as a dog run. ⊠ *Pacsirtamező u. at the junc-
tion where it meets Bécsi út.*

Zichy Kúria (Zichy Mansion). One wing of the Zichy Mansion is taken up by the **Óbudai Múzeum** (Óbuda Museum); permanent exhibitions here include traditional rooms
from typical homes in the district of Békásmegyer and a popular exhibit covering the history of toys from 1860 to
1960. Another wing houses the **Kassák Múzeum,** which honors the literary and artistic works of a pioneer of the Hungarian avant-garde, Lajos Kassák. ⊠ *Zichy Mansion, Fő
tér 1. Óbuda Museum:* ☎ *1/250–1020.* ▦ *100 Ft.* ☉ *Mid-
Mar.–mid-Oct., Tues.–Fri. 2–6, weekends 10–6; mid-
Oct.–mid-Mar. Tues.–Fri. 2–5, weekends 10–5. Kassák
Museum:* ☎ *1/368–7021.* ▦ *50 Ft.* ☉ *Oct.–Feb., Tues.–
Sun. 10–4; Mar.–Sept., Tues.–Sun. 10–6.*

3 Dining

IN BUDAPEST, there is a good selection of restaurants, from the grander establishments that echo the imperial past of the Hapsburg era to the less expensive, rustic spots favored by locals. In addition to trying out the standard *vendéglő* or *étterem* (restaurants), you can eat at an *önkiszolgáló étterem* (self-service restaurant), a *bistró étel bár* (sit-down snack bar), a *büfé* (snack counter), an *eszpresszó* (café), or a *söröző* (pub). And no matter how strict your diet, don't pass up a visit to at least one *cukrászda* (pastry shop).

Although prices are steadily increasing, there are plenty of good, affordable restaurants offering a variety of Hungarian dishes. Even in Budapest, eating out can provide you with some of the best value for the money of any European capital. In almost all restaurants, an inexpensive prix-fixe lunch called a *menü* is available, usually for as little as 350 Ft. It includes soup or salad, an entrée, and a dessert. One caveat: Some of the more touristy restaurants sometimes follow the international practice of embellishing tourists' bills; it doesn't hurt to check the prices discreetly before ordering and the total before paying. Budapest made international news last year for a flagrant overcharging incident; authorities have since cracked down on the guilty establishments. Don't order from menus without prices, and don't accept dining or drinking invitations from women hired to lure people into shady situations. Also note that many restaurants have a fine-print policy of charging for each slice of bread consumed from the bread basket.

Numerous new ethnic restaurants—from Chinese to Mexican to Hare Krishna Indian—are springing up all the time. The pulse of the city's increasingly vibrant restaurant scene is in downtown Pest; restaurants on Castle Hill tend to be more touristy and expensive. Our choice of restaurants is primarily Hungarian and Continental, but if you get a craving for sushi or tortellini, consult the restaurant listings in the English-language publications for the latest information on what's cooking where.

Hungarians eat early—you risk offhand service and cold food after 9 PM. Lunch, the main meal for many, is served from noon to 2. At most moderately priced and inexpensive restaurants, casual but neat dress is acceptable. Addresses below are preceded by the district number (in Roman numerals) and include the Hungarian postal code. Districts V, VI, and VII are in downtown Pest; I includes Castle Hill, the main tourist district of Buda. For information about Hungarian cuisine, *see* Pleasures and Pastimes *in* Chapter 1.

CATEGORY	COST*
$$$$	over 3,200 Ft.
$$$	2,300 Ft.–3,200 Ft.
$$	1,400 Ft.–2,300 Ft.
$	under 1,400 Ft.

*per person for a three-course meal, excluding drinks and gratuities

Castle Hill

$$$$ ✕ **Alabárdos.** As medieval as its name, the Halberdier (the wielder of that ancient weapon, the halberd), this vaulted wooden room in a 400-year-old Gothic house sits across from the Matthias Church. It has only a handful of tables, set with exquisite Herend and Zsolnay porcelain, though in summer a courtyard garden doubles its capacity. The impeccable service, flowery decor, quiet music, and overriding discretion make this an excellent place for a serious business meal. For extra flare, order the popular flambéed mixed grill: waiters turn the room's lights off before delivering it to your table. Late lunchers and early diners should note that Alabárdos is closed between 4 and 7 PM. ⊠ *I, Országház u. 2,* ☎ *1/356–0851. Reservations essential. Jacket and tie. AE, DC, MC, V. Closed Sun. No lunch mid-Oct.–mid-Apr.*

Downtown Pest and the Kis körút (Little Ring Road)

$$$–   ✕ **Múzeum.** The gustatory anticipation sparked by this el-
$$$$ egant, candlelit salon with mirrors, mosaics, and swift-moving waiters is matched by wholly satisfying, wonderful food. The salads are generous, the Hungarian wines excellent, and the chef dares to be creative. ⊠ *VIII, Múzeum körút 12,* ☎ *1/267–0375. Jacket and tie. AE. Closed Sun.*

$$$ ✕ **Lou Lou.** This glowing bistro tucked onto a side street
★ near the Danube has been the hottest restaurant in Buda-
pest for years. Blending local and Continental cuisines, the
menu includes a succulent fresh salmon with lemongrass;
the venison fillet with wild berry sauce is another mouth-
watering choice. At press time, Lou Lou was planning to
relocate to a larger space in fall 1998; check with Tourin-
form (☞ Visitor Information *in* Essential Information) for
the latest information. The restaurant closes between 3 PM
and 7 PM. ⊠ *V, Vigyázó Ferenc u. 4,* ☎ *1/312–4505.*
Reservations essential. AE. Closed Sat. lunch and Sun.

$$$ ✕ **Művészinas.** Walls hung with framed vintage prints and
★ photos, antique vitrines filled with old books, and tall,
slender candles on the tables create a romantic haze here.
Dozens of Hungarian specialties fill the long menu; beef,
veal, and poultry are each prepared a half dozen ways, from
sirloin "Budapest style" (smothered in a goose-liver, mushrooms, and sweet-pepper ragout) to spinach-stuffed turkey
breast in garlic sauce. Poppy-seed palacsinta with plum sauce
are a sublime dessert. ⊠ *VI, Bajcsy-Zsilinszky út 9,* ☎ *1/
268–1439. Reservations essential. AE, MC, V.*

$$ ✕ **Amstel River Café.** Just steps from the tourist-filled Váci
utca, you'll find this welcoming, low-key Dutch pub. The
menu has something for everyone—from rabbit to Caesar
salad to grilled chicken. Besides the Amstel beers (of course),
there's a weekly changing wine list. The breakfast menu—
a rarity in Budapest—has everything from corn flakes to
omelets to cold goose liver. ⊠ *V, Párizsi u. 6,* ☎ *1/266–
4334. No credit cards.*

$$ ✕ **Cyrano.** This smooth young bistro just off Vörösmarty
★ tér has an arty, contemporary bent, with wrought-iron
chairs, green-marble floors, and long-stemmed azure glasses.
The creative kitchen sends out elegantly presented Hungarian
and Continental dishes, from standards such as goulash and
chicken *paprikás* to more eclectic tastes like tender fried
Camembert cheese with blueberry jam. ⊠ *V, Kristóf tér 7–
8,* ☎ *1/266–3096. Reservations essential. AE, DC, MC.*

$$ ✕ **Duna-Corso.** Having stood on this riverfront square for
nearly two decades, this restaurant continues to offer good,
solid food at reasonable prices right in the center of Pest's
luxury-hotel belt. The bean-and-cabbage soup (laced with
smoked pork), roast duck with sauerkraut, and goose

Cafe NY
9-11 am K

Vkor Cafe ⊛
17 Sas Utca ✗

Legrody ⊛
near #14

Karpatia
(near about in
airline mag)
near german
church

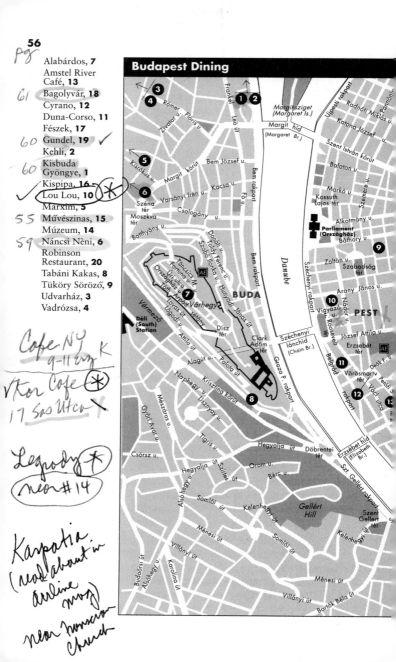

Budapest Dining

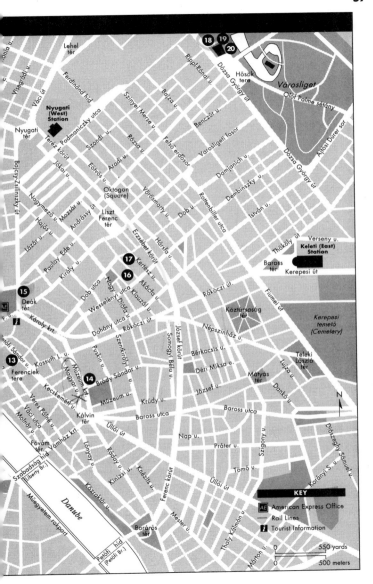

Lehel tér

Ferdinánd híd

Váci út

Szinyei Merse u.

Rippl-Rónai u.

Dózsa György út

18 **19**
20

Hősök tere

Városliget

Olof Palme sétány

Andrássy út

Nyugati (West) Station

Nyugati tér

Teréz körút

Podmaniczky utca

Szondi u.

Rózsa u.

Bajza u.

Benczúr u.

Felső erdősor

Városligeti fasor

Dózsa György út

Ajtósi Dürer sor

Bajcsy-Zsilinszky út

Jókai u.

Eötvös u.

Aradi u.

Nagymező u.

Mozsár u.

Andrássy út

Oktogon (Square)

Vörösmarty u.

Dob u.

Damjanich u.

Rottenbiller utca

Dembinszky u.

István u.

László u.

Hajós u.

Paulay Ede u.

Liszt Ferenc tér

Erzsébet körút

Hársfa u.

Thököly út

Verseny u.

Keleti (East) Station

Baross tér

Kerepesi út

Fiumei út

Dob utca

Nagy Diófa u.

Akácfa u.

Kertész u.

Klauzál u.

17
16

15
Deák tér

Wesselényi utca

Dohány utca

Rákóczi út

Rákóczi út

Köztársaság tér

Népszínház u.

Kerepesi temető (Cemetery)

Károly krt.

Puskin u.

Szentkirályi u.

József körút

Somogyi Béla u.

Berkocsis u.

Teleki László tér

Luca u.

Petőfi Sándor u.

Kossuth L. u.

Magyar u.

Bródy Sándor u.

Déri Miksa u.

Dankó u.

13
Ferenciek tere

Kecskeméti u.

Múzeum krt.

Múzeum u.

Krúdy u.

József u.

Mátyás tér

14

Veres Pálné u.

Kálvin tér

Baross utca

Baross utca

Molnár u.

Váci u.

Üllői út

Nap u.

Szigony u.

Diószeghy Sámuel u.

Fővám tér

Vámház krt.

Lónyay u.

Ráday u.

Práter u.

Szabadság híd (Liberty Br.)

Kinizsi u.

Közraktár u.

Tömő u.

Üllői út

Thaly Kálmán u.

Morton u.

Danube

Műegyetem rakpart

Bakáts u.

Ferenc körút

Mester u.

Boráros tér

N

KEY

AE American Express Office

Rail Lines

i Tourist Information

0 ___ 550 yards

0 ___ 500 meters

Petőfi híd (Petőfi Br.)

cracklings with potatoes are as simple and hearty as ever, and the service is still pokey and friendly. For views of the castle and Chain Bridge, a table on the vast outdoor terrace is the best seat in town. ⊠ *V, Vigadó tér 3,* ☎ *1/318–6362. No credit cards.*

$ ✕ **Fészek.** Hidden away inside the nearly 100-year-old Fészek Artists' Club is this large, neoclassical dining room. Inside it has high ceilings and mustard-color walls trimmed with ornate moldings, but if you come on a warm day, you can eat in a beautiful Venetian-style courtyard, originally monks' cloisters, with colorful majolica decorations and chestnut trees. The extensive menu features all the heavy Hungarian classics, with such specialties as turkey stuffed with goose liver and a variety of game dishes. You'll have to pay a 150-Ft. Artists' Club cover charge upon entering the building; if you've reserved a table in advance, it will be charged to your bill instead. ⊠ *VII, Kertész u. 36 (corner of Dob u.),* ☎ *1/322–6043. AE, DC, MC, V.*

$ ✕ **Kispipa.** Under the same management as Fészek (☞ *above*), this tiny, well-known restaurant with arched yellow-glass windows and piano bar features a similar, expansive menu of first-rate Hungarian food; the venison ragout soup with tarragon is excellent. ⊠ *VII, Akácfa u. 38,* ☎ *1/342–2587. Reservations essential. AE, MC. Closed Sun. and July–Aug.*

$ ✕ **Tüköry Söröző.** Hearty, decidedly nonvegetarian Hungarian fare comes in big portions at this popular spot close to Parliament. Best bets include pork cutlets stuffed with savory liver or apples and cheese, paired with a big mug of inexpensive beer. Courageous carnivores can sample the beefsteak tartare, topped with a raw egg. ⊠ *V, Hold u. 15,* ☎ *1/269–5027. MC, V. Closed weekends.*

North Buda

$$$$ ✕ **Vadrózsa.** The "Wild Rose" always has fresh ones on the table; the restaurant is in a romantic old villa perched on a hilltop in the exclusive Rózsadomb district of Buda. It's elegant to the last detail, with white-glove service, and the garden is delightful in summer. Try the venison or grilled fish; the house specialty, grilled goose liver, is succulent perfection. ⊠ *II. Pentelei Molnár u. 15,* ☎ *1/326–5817. Reservations essential. AE, DC, MC, V.*

$$$– ✕ **Udvarház.** The views from this Buda hilltop restaurant
$$$$ are unsurpassed. As you dine indoors at tables set with white linens or outdoors on the open terrace, your meals are accompanied by vistas of the Danube bridges and Parliament far below. Excellent fresh fish is prepared tableside; you could also try veal and goose liver in paprika sauce, served with salty cottage cheese dumplings. Catering to the predominantly tourist crowd, folklore shows and live Gypsy music frequently enliven the scene. The buses up here are infrequent; it's easier to take a car or taxi. ⊠ *III, Hármashatárhegyi út 2,* ☎ *1/388–6921. AE, DC, MC, V. Closed Mon. Nov.–Mar. No lunch weekdays Nov.–Mar.*

$$ ✕ **Náncsi Néni.** Aunt Nancy's restaurant is a perennial fa-
★ vorite, despite its out-of-the-way location. Irresistibly cozy, the dining room feels like Grandma's country kitchen: Chains of paprika and garlic dangle from the low wooden ceiling above tables set with red-and-white gingham tablecloths and fresh bread tucked into tiny baskets. Shelves along the walls are crammed with jars of home-pickled vegetables, which you can purchase to take home. On the home-style Hungarian menu (large portions!) turkey dishes feature a creative flair, such as breast fillets stuffed with apples, peaches, mushrooms, cheese, and sour cream. Special touches include a popular outdoor garden in summer and free champagne for all couples in love. ⊠ *II, Ördögárok út 80,* ☎ *1/397–2742. Reservations essential July–Aug. AE, MC, V.*

$ ✕ **Marxim.** Two years after the death of socialism in Hungary, this simple pizza-and-pasta restaurant opened up to mock the old regime—and milk it for all it's worth. From the flashing red star above the door outside to the photos of decorated hard-liners on the walls, the theme is "Communist nostalgia." Crowds of teenagers and blaring rock music make Marxim best suited for a lunch or snack. ⊠ *II, Kisrókus u. 23,* ☎ *1/212–4183. AE, DC, MC, V. No lunch Sun.*

Óbuda

$$$ ✕ **Kehli.** This pricey but laid-back, sepia-toned neighborhood tavern is on a hard-to-find street near the Óbuda end of the Árpád Bridge. The food is hearty and heavy, just the way legendary Hungarian writer and voracious eater Gyula Krúdy (to whom the restaurant is dedicated) liked it when he lived in the neighborhood. Select from appetizers, such as hot bone marrow with garlic toast, before moving on to fried goose livers with mashed potatoes or turkey breast stuffed with cheese and goose liver. ⊠ *III, Mókus utca 22,* ☎ *1/250–4241 or 1/368–0613. AE, MC, V. No lunch weekdays.*

$$$ ✕ Kisbuda Gyöngye. Considered one of the city's finest
★ restaurants, this intimate Óbuda restaurant is filled with antique furniture, and its walls are creatively decorated with an eclectic but elegant patchwork of carved wooden cupboard doors and panels. Try the venison with Transylvanian mushrooms or the popular *liba lakodalmas* (goose wedding feast), a roast goose leg, goose liver, and goose cracklings. ⊠ *III, Kenyeres u. 34,* ☎ *1/368–6402 or 1/368–9246. Reservations essential. AE, DC, MC, V. Closed Sun.*

Tabán and Gellért Hill

$$ ✕ Tabáni Kakas. This popular restaurant just below Castle Hill has a distinctly friendly atmosphere and specializes in large helpings of poultry dishes, particularly goose. Try the catfish *paprikás* or the roast duck with steamed cabbage. ⊠ *I, Attila út 27,* ☎ *1/375–7165. AE, MC, V.*

Városliget (City Park)

$$$$ ✕ Gundel. George Lang, Hungary's best-known restaura-
★ teur, showcases his native country's cuisine at this turn-of-the-century palazzo. Dark-wood paneling, a dozen oil paintings by exemplary Hungarian artists, and tables set with Zsolnay porcelain make this the city's plushest, most handsome dining room. Violinist György Lakatos, of the legendary Lakatos Gypsy musician dynasty, strolls from table to table playing folk music, as waiters in black tie serve traditional favorites such as tender veal in a paprika-and-sour-cream sauce and carp *Dorozsma* (panfried with mushrooms). ⊠ *XIV, Állatkerti út 2,* ☎ *1/321–3550. Reservations essential. Jacket and tie. AE, DC, MC, V.*

$$$$ ✕ **Robinson Restaurant.** At this intimate dining room on
the park's small lake, service is doting and the menu creative, with dishes such as crisp roast sucking pig with
champagne-drenched cabbage or fresh *fogas* (pike-perch)
stuffed with spinach. Finish it off with a flaming cup of coffee *Diablo*, fueled with Grand Marnier. Padded pastel decor
and low lighting wash the room in pleasant, if not Hungarian, elegance. ⊠ *XIV, Városliget,* ☎ *1/343–0955. Reservations essential. Jacket and tie. AE, DC, MC, V. Closed
daily 4–6 PM.*

$$ ✕ **Bagolyvár.** George Lang opened this restaurant next
★ door to his gastronomic palace, Gundel (☞ *above*), in
1993. The informal yet polished dining room has a soar-
ing wooden-beam ceiling, and the kitchen produces first-
rate daily menus of home-style Hungarian specialties.
Soups, served in shiny silver tureens, are particularly good.
Musicians entertain with cimbalom music nightly from 7
PM. In warm weather there is outdoor dining in a lovely back
garden. ⊠ *XIV, Állatkerti út 2,* ☎ *1/343–0217. AE, DC,
MC, V.*

4 Lodging

BUDAPEST IS WELL EQUIPPED with hotels and hostels, but the increase in tourism since 1989 has put a strain on the city's often crowded lodgings. Advance reservations are strongly advised, especially at the lower-price hotels. In winter it's not difficult to find a hotel room, even at the last minute, and prices are usually reduced by 20%–30%. By far the cheapest and most accessible beds in the city are rooms ($20–$25 for a double room) in private homes. Although most tourist offices book private rooms, the supply is limited, so try to arrive in Budapest early in the morning.

For single rooms with bath, count on paying about 80% of the double-room rate. During the off-season (September through March), rates can drop considerably. Note that most large hotels require payment in hard currency (either U.S. dollars or Deutschemarks). Addresses below are preceded by the district number (in Roman numerals) and include the Hungarian postal code. Districts V, VI, and VII are in downtown Pest; I includes Castle Hill, the main tourist district of Buda. For more about accommodations in Budapest, *see* Pleasures and Pastimes *in* Chapter 1.

CATEGORY	COST
$$$$	over $200
$$$	$140–$200
$$	$80–$140
$	under $80

All prices are for a standard double room with bath and breakfast during peak season (June through August).

$$$$ **Atrium Hyatt.** The spectacular 10-story interior—a mix of glass capsule elevators, cascading tropical greenery, an open bar, and café—is surpassed only by the views across the Danube to the castle (rooms with a river view cost substantially more). After major renovations, rooms have been tastefully redesigned with classy, unobtrusive decor in muted blues and light woods, and sparkling bathrooms. ⊠ *V, Roosevelt tér 2, H-1051,* ☎ *1/266–1234,* FAX *1/266–9101. 328 rooms, 27 suites. 3 restaurants, 2 bars, air-conditioning, in-room modem lines, no-smoking rooms, indoor pool, beauty salon, sauna, exercise room, casino, business services, meeting rooms, travel services, parking (fee). AE, DC, MC, V.*

64

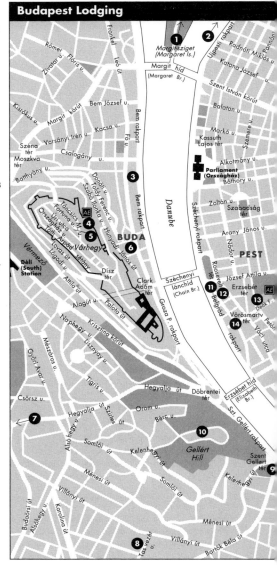

Budapest Lodging

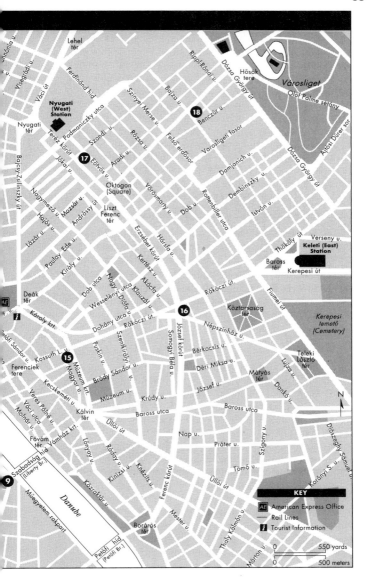

Lehel
tér

Ripoll Rónai u.

Dózsa György út

Hősök
tere

Városliget

Olof Palme sétány

Viserádi u.

Ferdinánd híd

Szinyei Merse u.

Bajza u.

Váci út

Nyugati
(West)
Station

Podmaniczky utca

18

Benczúr u.

Nyugati
tér

Teréz körút

Szondi u.

Rózsa u.

Felső erdősor

Városligeti fasor

Dózsa György út

Aytai Dürer sor

Bajcsy-Zsilinszky u.

17

Aradi u.

Eötvös u.

Jókai u.

Nagymező u.

Mozsár u.

Oktogon
(Square)

Vörösmarty u.

Dob u.

Rottenbiller utca

Hajós u.

Andrássy út

Liszt
Ferenc
tér

Domjánich u.

Dembinszky u.

István u.

Lázár u.

Paulay Ede u.

Erzsébet körút

Hársfa u.

Thököly u.

Verseny u.

Keleti (East)
Station

Király u.

Kertész u.

Baross
tér

Kerepesi út

Deák
tér

Dob utca

Nagy Diófa u.

Akácfa u.

Klauzál u.

Rákóczi út

Fiumei út

Kerepesi
temető
(Cemetery)

AE

Károly krt.

Wesselényi utca

Dohány utca

16

Köztársaság
tér

Petőfi Sándor u.

Károly krt.

i

Puskin u.

Szentkirályi u.

Rákóczi út

Nyár u.

Somogyi Béla u.

József körút

Népszinház u.

15

Kossuth L. u.

Múzeum krt.

Magyar u.

Bérkocsis u.

Teleki
László
tér

Ferenciek
tere

Kecskeméti u.

Brody Sándor u.

Déri Miksa u.

Mátyás
tér

Luza u.

Danko u.

Veres Pálné u.

Váci utca

Múzeum u.

Krúdy u.

József u.

Molnár u.

Kálvin
tér

Baross utca

Baross utca

N

Fővám
tér

Szabadság
(Liberty Br.)

Vámház krt.

Üllői út

Nap u.

Práter u.

Szigony u.

Diószeghy Sámuel u.

Lónyay u.

Ráday u.

Kinizsi u.

Krúsics u.

Tömő u.

Korányi S. u.

9

Danube

Műegyetem rakpart

Közraktár u.

Ferenc körút

Üllői út

Mester u.

Thaly Kálmán u.

Morton u.

Boráros
tér

Petőfi híd
(Petőfi Br.)

KEY

AE American Express Office

— Rail Lines

i Tourist Information

0 — 550 yards
0 — 500 meters

$$$$ 🏨 **Budapest Hilton.** Built in 1977 around a 13th-century
★ monastery adjacent to the Matthias Church, this perfectly
integrated architectural wonder overlooks the Danube from
the choicest site on Castle Hill. Every contemporary room
has a remarkable view; Danube vistas cost more. Complete
renovations during 1999 promise a welcome update in
room decor. Children, regardless of age, get free accom-
modation when sharing a room with their parents. Note:
Breakfast is not included in room rates. ✉ I, Hess András
tér 1–3, H-1014, ☎ 1/214–3000, 800/445–8667 in the
U.S. and Canada, FAX 1/356–0285. 295 rooms, 27 suites.
3 restaurants, 2 bars, café, wine cellar, air-conditioning, in-
room modem lines, beauty salon, sauna, exercise room,
casino, laundry services and dry cleaning, business services, meeting rooms, travel services, parking (free and
fee). AE, DC, MC, V.

$$$$ 🏨 **Budapest Marriott.** In this sophisticated yet friendly
★ hotel on the Danube in downtown Pest, attention to detail
is evident, from the impeccable buffet of colorfully glazed
pastries to the feather-light ring of the front-desk bell.
Guest rooms have lushly patterned carpets, floral bed-
spreads, and etched glass. The layout takes full advantage
of the hotel's prime Danube location, offering breathtaking views of Gellért Hill, the Chain and Elizabeth bridges,
and Castle Hill from the lobby, ballroom, every guest room,
and even the impressive health club—which is unques-
tionably the best hotel fitness center in the city. ✉ V,
Apáczai Csere János u. 4, H-1364, ☎ 1/266–7000, 800/
831–4004 in the U.S. and Canada, FAX 1/266–5000. 362
rooms, 20 suites. 3 restaurants, bar, air-conditioning, in-
room modem lines, no-smoking rooms, health club, squash,
shops, baby-sitting, laundry service and dry cleaning, business services, meeting rooms, travel services, parking (fee).
AE, DC, MC, V.

$$$$ 🏨 **Danubius Hotel Gellért.** The double-deck rotunda of
this grand Hungarian spa hotel leads you to expect a string
orchestra playing "The Emperor Waltz." Built in 1918, the
Jugendstil Gellért was favored by Otto von Habsburg, son
of the last emperor. Rooms come in all shapes and sizes—
from palatial suites to awkward, tiny spaces. Now part of
the Danubius hotel chain, the Gellért began an ambitious
three- to four-year overhaul in 1998—including the addi-

tion of air-conditioning and refurnishing of all rooms in the mood of the original Jugendstil style. The best views—across the Danube or up Gellért Hill—are more expensive; avoid those that face the building's inner core. Though the hotel's service can be a bit inconsistent, its famous pièce de résistance will make up for it: the monumental, ornate thermal baths. Admission to the spa is free to hotel guests (medical treatments cost extra); corridors and an elevator lead directly to the baths from the second, third, and fourth floors. ⊠ *XI, Gellért tér 1, H-1111,* ☎ *1/385–2200,* FAX *1/466–6631. 199 rooms, 13 suites. Restaurant, bar, brasserie, café, no-smoking rooms, indoor pool, beauty salon, spa, baby-sitting, business services, meeting rooms, parking (fee). AE, DC, MC, V.*

$$$$ 🏨 **Hotel Inter-Continental Budapest.** Formerly the Fórum ★ Hotel, this boxy, modern, riverside hotel consistently wins applause for its gracious appointments, excellent service, and gorgeous views across the Danube to Castle Hill. Sixty percent of the rooms have river views (these are more expensive); rooms on higher floors ensure the least noise. The hotel café, Bécsi Kávéház, is locally known for its pastries. The central location and efficient business services make the Inter-Continental popular with businesspeople. Note: Breakfast is not included in the room rates. ⊠ *V, Apáczai Csere János u. 12–14, Box 231, H-1368,* ☎ *1/327–6333,* FAX *1/327–6357. 392 rooms, 16 suites. 2 restaurants, bar, café, air-conditioning, in-room modem lines, no-smoking floors, pool, health club, business center, meeting rooms, car rental, parking (fee). AE, DC, MC, V.*

$$$$ 🏨 **Kempinski Hotel Corvinus Budapest.** Opened in August ★ 1992, this sleek luxury hotel is the favored lodging of visiting VIPs—from rock superstars to business moguls. From overnight shoe-shine service to afternoon chamber music in the lobby, the Kempinski exudes solicitousness. Unlike those of other nearby hotels, rooms are spacious, with blond and black Swedish geometric inlaid woods and an emphasis on functional touches, such as three phones in every room. Large, sparkling bathrooms, most with tubs and separate shower stalls and stocked with every toiletry, are the best in Budapest. The hotel's business services also stand out as the city's best. An automatic current in the smallish pool allows you to swim long distances without getting anywhere. Breakfast is not included in the room rates. ✉ *V, Erzsébet tér 7–8, H-1051,* ☎ *1/266–1000, 800/426–3135 in the U.S. and Canada,* 𝖥𝖠𝖷 *1/266–2000. 337 rooms, 28 suites. 2 restaurants, bar, lobby lounge, pub, air-conditioning, in-room modem lines, no-smoking rooms, indoor pool, barbershop, beauty salon, massage, health club, shops, laundry service and dry cleaning, business services, meeting rooms, travel services, parking (fee). AE, DC, MC, V.*

$$$ ⊞ **Danubius Grand Hotel Margitsziget.** Built in 1873 and long in disrepair, this venerable hotel reopened in 1987 as a Ramada Inn and was recently taken over by the Danubius hotel chain. Room rates may have increased since the 1870s, but the high ceilings haven't been lowered. Nor have the old-fashioned room trimmings—down comforters, ornate chandeliers—been lost in the streamlining. Choose between views across the Danube onto a less attractive, industrial section of Pest or out onto the verdant lawns and trees of a tranquil park. Because it's connected to a bubbling thermal spa next door and is located on car-free Margaret Island in the Danube right between Buda and Pest, the Danubius Grand feels removed from the city but is still only a short taxi or bus ride away. ✉ *XIII, Margit-sziget, H-1138,* ☎ *1/329–2300 or 1/349–2769 (reservations),* 𝖥𝖠𝖷 *1/353–3029. 164 rooms, 10 suites. 2 restaurants, no-smoking rooms, indoor pool, beauty salon, massage, spa, sauna, exercise room, bicycles, meeting rooms, travel services, free parking. AE, DC, MC, V.*

$$$ ⊞ **Danubius Thermal Hotel Helia.** A sleek Scandinavian design and less hectic location upriver from downtown make this spa hotel on the Danube a change of pace from its Pest peers. Its neighborhood is nondescript, but guests can be in town in minutes or take advantage of the thermal baths and special health packages—including everything from Turkish baths to electrotherapy and fitness tests. The staff is friendly and helpful, and most of the comfortable rooms have Danube views. ✉ *XIII, Kárpát u. 62–64, H-1133,* ☎ *1/270–3277,* 𝖥𝖠𝖷 *1/270–2262. 254 rooms, 8 suites. Restaurant, bar, café, indoor pool, beauty salon, hot tub, massage, sauna, spa, steam room, tennis courts, exercise room, business services, meeting rooms, free parking. AE, DC, MC, V.*

$$$ 🏨 **Flamenco.** Classy though sometimes overlooked, this hotel in the Buda foothills is a welcome addition to this side of the river. A wall of windows in the low-ceilinged lobby opens out onto views of a park. Service is professional, and the well-kept contemporary rooms are priced at the lowest end of this category. ⊠ *XI, Tas Vezér utca 7, H–1113,* ☎ *1/372–2068 or* ☎ *1/372–2000,* 🖷 *1/372–2100. 352 rooms, 8 suites. 2 restaurants, indoor pool, beauty salon, sauna, business services, meeting rooms, travel services, parking (fee). AE, DC, MC, V.*

$$$ 🏨 **Radisson SAS Béke.** The well-situated Béke (on a main boulevard near the Nyugati [West] Railroad Station) is a budget family inn turned luxury hotel—it now has a glittering turn-of-the-century facade, a lobby lined with mosaics and statuary, and bellmen bowing before the grand marble staircase. Guest rooms resemble solidly modern living rooms, with two-tone wood furnishings and pastel decor. ⊠ *VI, Teréz krt. 43, H-1067,* ☎ *1/301–1600,* 🖷 *1/301–1615. 238 rooms, 8 suites. 2 restaurants, 2 bars, café, air-conditioning, in-room modem lines, no-smoking rooms, pool, beauty salon, sauna, casino, business center, meeting rooms, travel services, parking (fee). AE, DC, MC, V.*

$$ 🏨 **Alba Hotel.** Tucked behind an alleyway at the foot of Castle Hill, this spotless, modern hotel is a short walk via the Chain Bridge from lively business and shopping districts. Rooms are snug and quiet, with clean white-and-pale-gray contemporary decor and charmingly typical Budapest views over a kaleidoscope of rooftops and chimneys. Half have bathtubs. ⊠ *I, Apor Péter u. 3, H-1011,* ☎ *1/375–9244,* 🖷 *1/375–9899. 95 rooms. Bar, breakfast room, air-conditioning, no-smoking rooms, meeting room, parking (fee). AE, DC, MC, V.*

$$ 🏨 **Astoria.** At a busy intersection in downtown Pest stands a revitalized turn-of-the-century hotel that remains an oasis of quiet in hectic surroundings. Staff members are always—but unobtrusively—on hand. Rooms are genteel, spacious, and comfortable, and renovations have remained faithful to the original decor: rather like Grandma's sitting room, in Empire style with an occasional antique. The Astoria's opulent café is a popular meeting place. ⊠ *V, Kossuth Lajos u. 19–21, H-1053,* ☎ *1/317–3411,* 🖷 *1/318–6798. 125 rooms, 5 suites. Restaurant, bar, café, no-smoking* *rooms, nightclub, business services, meeting rooms, free parking. AE, DC, MC, V.*

$$ 🔲 **Hotel Centrál.** Relive history—stay in this hotel, well situated in a leafy diplomatic quarter just one block from Heroes' Square, as visiting Communist dignitaries once did. The architecture and furnishings are straight out of the 1950s, but rooms are comfortable and most have unusually large bathrooms. Suites, however, as well as six of the standard rooms, are classically elegant, with turn-of-the-century Hungarian furnishings; ask for the suite that was Rudolf Nureyev's favorite. ⊠ *VI, Munkácsy Mihály u. 5–7, H-1063,* 🕾 *1/321–2000,* ℻ *1/322–9445. 36 rooms, 6 suites. Restaurant, free parking. AE, MC, V.*

$$ 🔲 **Nemzeti.** With a lovely, baby-blue Baroque facade, the Nemzeti reflects the grand mood of the turn of the century. The high-ceiling lobby and public areas—with pillars, arches, and wrought-iron railings—are elaborately elegant. A timely renovation begun in late 1997 is transforming the once small, dark, unexceptional guest rooms with pretty, new furnishings and air-conditioning; be sure to ask for one of these rooms (20 DM extra) for optimal comfort. The hotel is located at bustling Blaha Lujza tér in the center of Pest, which tends toward the seedy after dark; although windows are double-paned, to ensure a quiet night, ask for a room facing the inner courtyard. ⊠ *VIII, József körút 4, H-1088,* 🕾 *1/303–9310,* ℻ *1/314–0019,* 🕾 ℻ *1/303–9162. 75 rooms, 1 suite. Restaurant, air-conditioning, piano bar, meeting room, travel services. AE, DC, MC, V.*

$$ 🔲 **Victoria.** The Parliament building and city lights twink-
★ ling over the river can be seen from the picture windows of every room at this young establishment right on the Danube. The tiny hotel mixes the charm of a small inn with the modern comforts and efficiency of a business hotel. The location—an easy walk from Castle Hill sights and downtown Pest—couldn't be better. ⊠ *I, Bem rakpart 11, H-1011,* 🕾 *1/457–8080,* ℻ *1/457–8088. 27 rooms, 1 suite. Bar, air-conditioning, sauna, meeting room, travel services, parking (fee). AE, DC, MC, V.*

$ 🔲 **Citadella.** Comparatively basic, the Citadella is nevertheless very popular for its price and for its stunning location—right inside the fortress. Half of the rooms compose a youth hostel, giving the hotel a lively communal atmosphere. None of the rooms have bathrooms, but half have showers. Breakfast is not included in the rates. ✉ *XI, Citadella sétány, Gellérthegy, H–1118,* ☎ *1/366–5794,* FAX *1/386–0505. 20 rooms, none with bath. Breakfast room. No credit cards.

$ ★ ⛏ **Kulturinov.** One wing of a magnificent 1902 neo-Baroque castle now houses basic budget accommodations. Rooms come with two or three beds and are clean and delightfully peaceful; they have showers but no tubs. The neighborhood—one of Budapest's most famous squares in the luxurious castle district—is magical. ✉ *I, Szentháromság tér 6, H–1014,* ☎ *1/355–0122 or 1/375–1651,* FAX *1/375–1886. 16 rooms. Snack bar, library, meeting rooms. AE, DC, MC, V.*

$ ⛏ **Molnár Panzió.** Fresh air and peace and quiet could lure you to this immaculate guest house nestled high above Buda on Széchenyi Hill. Rooms in the octagonal main house are polyhedric, clean, and bright, with pleasant wood paneling and pastel-color modern furnishings; most have distant views of Castle Hill and Gellért Hill, and some have balconies. Eight rooms in a new (1997) addition next door are more private and have superior bathrooms. Breakfast here is more appealing than usual—with scrambled eggs in addition to the standard breads and jams. ✉ *XII, Fodor u. 143, H–1124,* ☎ *1/395–1873,* ☎ FAX *1/395–1872. 23 rooms. Restaurant, bar, sauna, exercise room, playground, travel services, free parking. AE, DC, MC, V.*

5 Nightlife and the Arts

BONUS MILES MAKE GREAT SOUVENIRS.

Earn Miles With Your MCI Card.

Take the MCI Card along on this trip and start earning miles for the next one. You'll earn frequent flyer miles on all your calls and save with the low rates you've come to expect from MCI. Before you know it, you'll be on your way to some other international destination.

Sign up for MCI by calling
1-800-FLY-FREE

Earn Frequent Flyer Miles.

Is this a great time, or what? :-)

MCI

Easy To Call Home.

1. To use your MCI Card, just dial the WorldPhone access number of the country you're calling from.
2. Dial or give the operator your MCI Card number.
3. Dial or give the number you're calling.

# Austria (CC) ♦	022-903-012
# Belarus (CC)	
From Brest, Vitebsk, Grodno, Minsk	8-800-103
From Gomel and Mogilev regions	8-10-800-103
# Belgium (CC) ♦	0800-10012
# Bulgaria	00800-0001
# Croatia (CC) ★	0800-22-0112
# Czech Republic (CC) ♦	00-42-000112
# Denmark (CC) ♦	8001-0022
# Finland (CC) ♦	08001-102-80
# France (CC) ♦	0-800-99-0019
# Germany (CC)	0800-888-8000
# Greece (CC) ♦	00-800-1211
# Hungary (CC) ♦	00▼800-01411
# Iceland (CC) ♦	800-9002
# Ireland (CC)	1-800-55-1001
# Italy (CC) ♦	172-1022
# Kazakhstan (CC)	8-800-131-4321
# Liechtenstein (CC) ♦	0800-89-0222
# Luxembourg	0800-0112
# Monaco (CC) ♦	800-90-019
# Netherlands (CC) ♦	0800-022-9122
# Norway (CC) ♦	800-19912
# Poland (CC) ⊹	00-800-111-21-22
# Portugal (CC) ⊹	05-017-1234
Romania (CC) ⊹	01-800-1800
# Russia (CC) ⊹ ♦	
To call using ROSTELCOM ■	747-3322
For a Russian-speaking operator	747-3320
To call using SOVINTEL ■	960-2222
# San Marino (CC) ♦	172-1022
# Slovak Republic (CC)	00-421-00112
# Slovenia	080-8808
# Spain (CC)	900-99-0014
# Sweden (CC) ♦	020-795-922
# Switzerland (CC) ♦	0800-89-0222
# Turkey (CC) ♦	00-8001-1177
# Ukraine (CC) ⊹	8▼10-013
# United Kingdom (CC)	
To call using BT ■	0800-89-0222
To call using C&W ■	0500-89-0222
# Vatican City (CC)	172-1022

CHASE

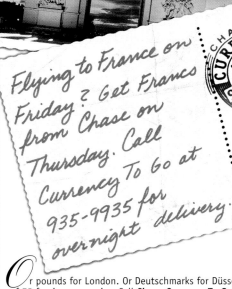

Flying to France on Friday? Get Francs from Chase on Thursday. Call Currency To Go at 935-9935 for overnight delivery.

CHASE CURRENCY TO GO 935-9935

*O*r pounds for London. Or Deutschmarks for Düsseldorf. Or any of 75 foreign currencies. Call **Chase Currency To Go**ˢᴹ at **935-9935** in area codes 212, 718, 914, 516 and Rochester, N.Y.; all other area codes call 1-800-935-9935. We'll deliver directly to your door.* Overnight. And there are no exchange fees. Let Chase make your trip an easier one.

CHASE. The right relationship is everything.ˢᴹ

The Arts

For the latest on arts events, consult the entertainment listings of the English-language newspapers (☞ English-Language Periodicals *in* Essential Information). Their weekly entertainment calendars map out all that's happening in Budapest's arts and culture world—from thrash bands in wild clubs to performances at the Opera House. Another option is to stop in at the **National Philharmonic ticket office** (⊠ Vörösmarty tér 1, ☎ 1/318–0281) and browse through the scores of free programs and fliers and scan the walls coated with upcoming concert posters. Hotels and tourist offices will also provide you with a copy of the monthly publication *Programme,* which contains details of all cultural events.

Tickets can be bought at the venues themselves, but many ticket offices sell them without extra charge. Prices are still very low, so markups of even 30% shouldn't dent your wallet if you book through your hotel. Inquire at Tourinform (☞ Visitor Information *in* Essential Information) if you're not sure where to go. Ticket availability depends on the performance and season—it's usually possible to get tickets a few days before a show, but performances by major international artists sell out early. Tickets to Budapest Festival Orchestra concerts and other festival events also go particularly quickly.

Theater and opera tickets are sold at the **Central Theater Booking Office** (Pest: ⊠ VI, Andrassy út 18, ☎ 1/312–0000). For classical concert, ballet, and opera tickets, as well as tickets for major pop and rock shows, go to the **National Philharmonic Ticket Office** (☞ *above*). **Music Mix Ticket Service** (⊠ V, Váci utca 33, ☎ 1/338–2237 or 1/317–7736) specializes in popular music but handles other genres as well.

CLASSICAL MUSIC AND OPERA

The tiny recital room of the **Bartók Béla Emlékház** (Bartók Béla Memorial House; ⊠ II, Csalán út 29, ☎ 1/376–2100) hosts intimate Friday evening chamber music recitals by well-known ensembles from mid-March to June and September to mid-December.

The **Budapest Kongresszusi Központ** (Budapest Convention Center; ⊠ XII, Jagelló út 1–3, ☎ 1/209–1990) is the city's largest-capacity (but least atmospheric) classical concert venue and usually hosts the largest-selling events of the Spring Festival.

The homely little sister of the Opera House, the **Erkel Színház** (Erkel Theater; ⌧ VII, Köztársaság tér 30, ☎ 1/333–0540) is Budapest's other main opera and ballet venue. There are no regular performances in the summer.

Liszt Ferenc Zeneakadémia (Franz Liszt Academy of Music; ⌧ VI, Liszt Ferenc tér 8, ☎ 1/342–0179), usually referred to as the Music Academy, is Budapest's premier classical concert venue, hosting orchestra and chamber music concerts in its splendid main hall. It's sometimes possible to grab a standing-room ticket just before a performance here.

The glittering **Magyar Állami Operaház** (Hungarian State Opera House; ⌧ VI, Andrassy út 22, ☎ 1/331–2550), Budapest's main venue for operas and classical ballet, presents an international repertoire of classical and modern works as well as such Hungarian favorites as Kodály's *Háry János*. Except during the one-week BudaFest international opera and ballet festival in mid-August, the Opera House is closed during the summer.

Colorful operettas like those by Lehár and Kalman are staged at their main Budapest venue, the **Operetta Theater** (⌧ VI, Nagymező u. 19, ☎ 1/332–0535); also look for modern dance productions and Hungarian renditions of popular Broadway classics.

Classical concerts are held regularly at the **Pesti Vigadó** (Pest Concert Hall; ⌧ V, Vigadó tér 2, ☎ 1/318–9167).

ENGLISH-LANGUAGE MOVIES

Many of the English-language movies that come to Budapest are subtitled in Hungarian rather than dubbed. There are more than 30 cinemas that regularly show films in English, and tickets are very inexpensive by Western standards (about 800 Ft.). Consult the movie matrix in the *Budapest Sun* or *Budapest Week* for a weekly list of what's showing.

FOLK DANCING

Many of Budapest's district cultural centers regularly hold traditional regional folk-dancing evenings, or dance houses (*táncház*), often with general instruction at the beginning. These sessions provide a less touristy way to taste Hungarian culture.

Almássy Recreation Center (⊠ VII, Almássy tér 6, ☎ 1/352–1572) holds numerous folk-dancing evenings, representing Hungarian as well as Greek and other ethnic cultures. Traditionally the wildest táncház is held Saturday nights at the **Inner City Youth and Cultural Center** (⊠ V, Molnár u. 9, ☎ 1/317–5928), where the stomping and whirling go on way into the night. Hungary's best-known folk ensemble, Muzsikás, hosts a weekly dance house at the **Marczibányi téri Művelődési ház** (Marczibányi tér Cultural Center; ⊠ II, Marczibányi tér 5/a, ☎ 1/212–5789), usually on Thursday nights. Muzsikás lead singer, Márta Sebestyén, appears less and less frequently with the group since her singing was featured in the movie *The English Patient*, launching her into international recognition; call ahead to find out when she'll perform next.

FOLKLORE PERFORMANCES

The **Hungarian State Folk Ensemble** performs regularly at the **Budai Vigadó** (⊠ I, Corvin tér 8, ☎ 1/201–5846); shows incorporate music, dancing, and singing.

The **Folklór Centrum** (⊠ XI, Fehérvári út 47, ☎ 1/203–3868) has been a major venue for folklore performances for more than 30 years. It hosts regular traditional folk concerts and dance performances from spring through fall.

THEATERS

The **Madách Theater** (⊠ VII, Erzsébet körút 31–33, ☎ 1/322–2015) produces colorful musicals in Hungarian, including a popular adaptation of *Cats*. English-language dramas are not common in Budapest, but when there are any, they are usually staged at the **Merlin Theater** (⊠ V, Gerlóczy utca 4, ☎ 1/317–9338). In summer, the Merlin usually hosts an English-language theater series. Another musical theater is the **Thália Theater** (⊠ VI, Nagymező u. 22–24, ☎ 1/331–0500). The sparkling **Vígszínház** (Comedy Theater; ⊠ XIII, Pannónia út 1, ☎ 1/269–5340) hosts

classical concerts and dance performances but is primarily
a venue for musicals, such as the Hungarian adaptation of
West Side Story.

Nightlife

Budapest's nightlife is vibrant and diverse. For basic beer
and wine drinking, *sörözős* (beer bars) and *borozős* (wine
bars) abound, although the latter tend to serve the early-
morning-spritzer-before-work types rather than nighttime
revelers. For quiet conversation there are *drink-bárs* in
most hotels and all over town, but beware of the inflated
prices and steep cover charges. Cafés are preferable for un-
escorted women.

Most nightspots and clubs have bars, pool tables, and dance
floors. Although some places do accept credit cards, it's best
to expect to pay cash for your night on the town. As is the
case in most other cities, the life of a club or disco in Budapest can be somewhat ephemeral. Those listed below are quite
popular and seem to be here to stay. But for the very latest
on the more transient "in" spots, consult the nightlife sections of the *Budapest Sun* and *Budapest Week.*

Budapest also has its share of seedy go-go clubs and so-called
"cabarets," some of which are known for scandalously
excessive billing and physical intimidation. Be wary if you
are "invited" in by women lingering nearby, and don't
order anything without first seeing the price.

A word of warning to the smoke-sensitive: Budapest is a
city of smokers. No matter where you spend your night out,
chances are you'll come home smelling of cigarette smoke.

BARS AND CLUBS

Angel Bar and Disco (✉ VII, Szövetség u. 33, ☎ 1/351–
6490) is one of Budapest's enduring and most popular gay
bars (though all persuasions are welcome), with a rollick-
ing dance floor. It's closed Monday–Wednesday.

Bahnhof (✉ VI, Váci út 1, at Nyugati pu.) is, appropriately,
in the Nyugati (Western) train station and attracts swarms
of young people to its large, crowded dance floor to live
bands and DJ'd music. It's closed Sunday–Tuesday.

The most popular of Budapest's Irish pubs and a favorite expat watering hole is **Becketts** (⊠ V, Bajcsy-Zsilinszky út 72, ☎ 1/311–1035), where Guinness flows freely and excellent Irish fare is served amid the gleams of polished wood and brass.

One of the city's hottest spots is **Café Capella** (⊠ V, Belgrád rakpart 23, ☎ 1/318–6231), where a welcoming, gay-friendly crowd flocks to the glittery drag shows (held a few times a week) and revels to DJ'd club music until dawn.

A hip, mellow crowd mingles at the stylish **Cafe Incognito** (⊠ VI, Liszt Ferenc tér 3, ☎ 1/351–9428), with low lighting and funky music kept at a conversation-friendly volume. Couches and armchairs in the back are comfy and private. It closes relatively early—at midnight.

Café Pierrot (⊠ I, Fortuna u. 14, ☎ 1/375–6971), an elegant café and piano bar on a small street on Castle Hill, is well suited to a secret rendezvous.

The look is sophisticated and stylish but the mood low-key and unpretentious at the **Fél 10 Jazz Club** (⊠ VIII, Baross u. 30, cellular ☎ 06–60/318-467), near Kálvin tér. Three open levels with balconylike sitting areas, a dance floor, and two bars are impeccably decorated with wrought-iron tables and maroon-cushioned chairs.

Established Hungarian jazz headliners and young up-and-comers play nightly at the **Long Jazz Club** (⊠ VII, Dohány u. 22–24, ☎ 1/322–0066). It's closed Sunday.

Housed in an old stone mansion near Heroes' Square, the conceptually schizophrenic **Made Inn** (⊠ VI, Andrássy út 112, ☎ 1/311–3437) has an elaborate decor modeled on an underground mine shaft, a kitchen specializing in Mediterranean foods, a large outdoor bar, and a disco dance floor packed with local and international Beautiful People with cell phones and fake-bake tans. Live bands play most nights.

Cool (and trendily dark) **Underground** (⊠ VI, Teréz krt. 30, ☎ 1/311–1481) is below the artsy Művész movie theater. Exposed metal beams and girders and wackily shaped scrap-metal chairs and tables give this bar the requisite industrial look; the DJ spins progressive popular music. Weekends are packed with younger, sometimes rowdy, hipsters.

CASINOS

Most casinos are open daily from 2 PM until 4 or 5 AM and offer gambling in hard currency—usually dollars—only.

The **Gresham Casino** (⊠ V, Roosevelt tér 5, ☎ 1/317–2407) is in the famous Gresham Palace at the Pest end of the Chain Bridge. Sylvester Stallone is alleged to be an owner of the popular **Las Vegas Casino** (⊠ V, Roosevelt tér 2, ☎ 1/317–6022), in the Atrium Hyatt Hotel. In an 1879 building designed by prolific architect Miklós Ybl, who also designed the State Opera House, the **Várkert Casino** (⊠ I, Miklós Ybl tér 9, ☎ 1/202–4244) is the most attractive of the city's casinos.

6 Shopping

YOU'LL FIND PLENTY of expensive boutiques, folk-art and souvenir shops,
foreign-language bookstores, and clas-
sical-record shops on or around touristy Váci utca, Budapest's famous, upscale pedestrian-only promenade. While
a stroll along **Váci utca** is integral to a Budapest visit,
browsing among some of the smaller, less touristy, more typically Hungarian shops in Pest—on the **Kis körút** (Little Ring
Road) and **Nagy körút** (Great Ring Road)—may prove
more interesting and less pricey. Lots of arty boutiques are
springing up in the section of District V **south of Ferenciek
tere and toward the Danube,** and around **Kálvin tér.** Charming **Falk Miksa utca,** also in the fifth district, running south
from Szent István körút, is one of the city's best antiques
districts, lined on both sides with atmospheric little shops
and galleries.

Department Stores

Skála Metro (⊠ VI, Nyugati tér 1–2, ☎ 1/353–2222), opposite the Nyugati (Western) Railroad Station, is one of the
largest and best-known department stores, selling a little
bit of not entirely everything. **Fontana,** on Váci utca, has
several floors of cosmetics, clothing, and other goods, all
with price tags reflecting the store's expensive address.

Markets

For true bargains and possibly an adventure, make an early
morning trip to the vast **Ecseri Piac** (⊠ IX, Nagykőrösi út;
take Bus 54 from Boráros tér), on the outskirts of the city.
A colorful, chaotic market that shoppers have flocked to
for decades, it is an arsenal of secondhand goods, where
you can find everything from frayed Russian army fatigues
to Herend and Zsolnay porcelain vases to antique silver chalices. Goods are sold at permanent tables set up in rows, from
trunks of cars parked on the perimeter, and by lone, shady
characters clutching just one or two items. As a foreigner,
you may be overcharged, so prepare to haggle—it's part

of the flea-market experience. Also, watch out for pick-pockets. Ecseri is open weekdays 8–4, Saturday 8–3, but the best selection is on Saturday mornings.

A colorful outdoor flea market is held weekend mornings from 7 to 2 at **Petőfi Csarnok** (✉ XIV, Városliget, Zichy Mihály út 14, ☎ 1/251–7266), in City Park. The quantity and selection are smaller than at Ecseri Piac, but it offers a fun flea-market experience closer to the city center. Many visitors buy red-star medals, Russian military watches, and other memorabilia from Communist days here. One other option is **Vásárcsarnok** (☞ Downtown Pest and the Kis körút *in* Chapter 2).

Specialty Stores

Antiques

Falk Miksa utca (☞ *above*), lined with antiques stores, is a delightful street for multiple-shop browsing.

The shelves and tables at tiny **Anna Antikvitás** (✉ V, Falk Miksa u. 18–20, ☎ 1/302–5461) are stacked with exquisite antique textiles—from heavily embroidered wall hangings to dainty lace gloves. Exquisite cloth and lace parasols line the ceiling, but these, unfortunately, are not for sale; similar ones are, however, sometimes available. The store also carries assorted antique objets d'art. **BÁV Mütárgy** (✉ V, Ferenciek tere 12, ☎ 1/318–3381; ✉ V, Kossuth Lajos u. 3, ☎ 1/318–4403; ✉ V, Szent István krt. 3, ☎ 1/331–4534), the State Commission Trading House, has antiques of all shapes, sizes, kinds, and prices at its several branches around the city. While they all have a variety of objects, porcelain is the specialty at the branch on Kossuth Lajos utca, and paintings at the Szent István körút store. **Polgár Galéria és Aukciósház** (✉ V, Kossuth Lajos u. 3, ☎ 1/318–6954) sells everything from jewelry to furniture and also holds several auctions a year. **Qualitás** (✉ V, Falk Miksa u. 32; ✉ V, Kígyó u. 5; ✉ VII, Dohány u. 1) sells paintings, furniture, and decorative objects at its branches around town.

Art Galleries

Budapest has dozens of art galleries showing and selling old works as well as the very latest. **Dovin Gallery** (✉ V, Galamb

u. 6, ☎ 1/318–3673) specializes in Hungarian contemporary paintings. New York celebrity Yoko Ono opened **Gallery 56** (✉ V, Falk Miksa u. 7, ☎ 1/269–2529) to show art by internationally famed artists, such as Keith Haring, as well as works by up-and-coming Hungarian artists. You can also visit **Mai Manó Fotógaléria** (☞ Andrássy út *in* Chapter 2).

Books

You'll encounter bookselling stands throughout the streets and metro stations of the city, many of which sell English-language souvenir picturebooks at discount prices. **Váci utca** is lined with bookstores that sell glossy coffee-table books about Budapest and Hungary.

Atlantisz (✉ V, Váci u. 31–33) has a selection of English classics, as well as academic texts. **Bestsellers** (✉ V, Október 6 u. 11, ☎ 1/312–1295) sells exclusively English-language books and publications, including best-selling paperbacks and a variety of travel guides about Hungary and beyond. The **Central European University Bookshop** (✉ V, Nádor u. 9, ☎ 1/327–3096), in the Central European University, is a more academically focused branch of Bestsellers bookstore. If you're interested in reading up on this part of the world, this is the store for you. You'll also find a good selection of books in English at **Idegennyelvű Könyvesbolt** (✉ V, Petőfi Sándor u. 2 [in Párisi udvar]), which specializes in foreign-language books. **Írók boltja** (Writers' Bookshop; ✉ VI, Andrássy út 45, ☎ 1/322–1645), one of Budapest's main literary bookstores, has a small but choice selection of Hungarian fiction and poetry translated into English. The hushed, literary atmosphere is tangible, and small tables are set out for reading and enjoying a cup of self-serve tea and instant coffee.

China, Crystal, and Porcelain

Hungary is famous for its age-old Herend porcelain, which is hand-painted in the village of Herend near Lake Balaton. For the Herend name and quality without the steep price tag, visit **Herend Village Pottery** (✉ II, Bem rakpart 37, ☎ 1/356–7899), where you can choose from Herend's practical line of durable ceramic cups, dishes, and table settings. The brand's Budapest store, **Herendi Porcelán Márkabolt** (✉ V, József Nádor tér 11, ☎ 1/317–2622), sells a variety of the delicate (and pricey) pieces, from figurines to dinner sets. Hungary's exquisite Zsolnay porcelain, created and hand-painted in Pécs, is sold at the **Zsolnay Márkabolt** (⊠ V, Kígyó u. 4, ☎ 1/318–3712).

Hungarian and Czech crystal is considerably less expensive here than in the United States. **Goda Kristály** (⊠ V, Váci u. 9, ☎ 1/318–4630) has beautiful colored and clear pieces. **Haas & Czjzek** (⊠ VI, Bajcsy-Zsilinszky út 23, ☎ 1/311–4094) has been in the business for more than 100 years, selling a variety of porcelain, glass, and ceramic pieces in traditional and contemporary styles. Crystal and porcelain dealers also sell their wares at the Ecseri Piac flea market (☞ Markets, *above*), often at discount prices, but those looking for authentic Herend and Zsolnay should beware of imitations.

Clothing

Fidji Boutique (⊠ V, Váci u. 30, ☎ 1/266–7113) has racks of snazzy men's clothes by international designers like Christian Dior. The **Hugo Boss Shop** (⊠ V, Erzsébet tér 7–8, ☎ 1/266–7867), in the Kempinski Hotel, has a good selection of men's suits. High-fashion women's outfits by top Hungarian designers are for sale at **Monarchia** (⊠ V, Szabadsajtó út 6, ☎ 1/318–3146), a tiny boutique with rich burgundy velvet draperies and ceilings higher than its floor space. **Manier** (⊠ V, Váci u. 48 [entrance at Nyári Pál u. 4], ☎ 1/318–1812) is a popular haute couture salon run by talented Hungarian designer Anikó Németh offering women's pieces ranging from quirky to totally outrageous. The store's second branch is across the street at Váci utca 53.

Folk Art

Handmade articles, such as embroidered tablecloths and painted plates, are sold all over the city by Transylvanian women wearing traditional scarves and colorful skirts. You can usually find them standing at **Moszkva tér, Jászai Mari tér,** outside the **Kossuth tér** metro, around **Váci utca,** and in the larger metro stations.

Éva Dolls (⊠ V, Kecskeméti u. 10, ☎ 1/266–5373), a small store near Kálvin tér, has pricey but beautiful crafts. All types of folk art—pottery, blouses, jewelry boxes, wood carvings, embroidery—can be purchased at one of the many branches of Népművészet Háziipar, also called **Folkart Centrum** (✉ V, Váci u. 14, ☎ 1/318–5840), a large cooperative chain. Prices are reasonable, and selection and quality are good. **Holló Műhely** (✉ V, Vitkovics Mihály u. 12, ☎ 1/317–8103) sells the work of László Holló, a master wood craftsman who has resurrected traditional motifs and styles of earlier centuries. There are lovely hope chests, chairs, jewelry boxes, candlesticks, and more, all hand-carved and hand-painted with cheery folk motifs—a predominance of birds and flowers in reds, blues, and greens.

Home Decor and Gifts

Bon-Bon (✉ VIII, Baross u. 4, ☎ no phone) is a cramped little boutique near Kálvin tér packed with bohemian beads and necklaces, handpressed paper and cards, colorful ceramic mugs, and various assorted knickknacks—all at very reasonable prices. **Hephaistos Háza** (✉ VI, Zichy Jenő u. 20, ☎ 1/332–6329) is one of Budapest's hottest interior design stores, selling tastefully eclectic wrought-iron furniture and accessories with its signature curlicue flourishes. You can commission an entire room's decor (many local restaurants and bars do) or, more realistically, take home a creative candleholder or two.

Music

Recordings of Hungarian folk music or of pieces played by Hungarian artists are increasingly available on compact discs, though cassettes and records are much cheaper and are sold throughout the city. CDs are normally quite expensive—about 4,000 Ft.

Amadeus (✉ V, Szende Pál u. 1, ☎ 1/318–6691), just off of the Duna korzó, has an extensive selection of classical CDs. **Hungaroton Hanglemez Szalon** (✉ V, Vörösmarty tér 1, ☎ 1/338–2810) has a large selection of all types of music and is centrally located. Its separate, extensive section on Hungarian artists is great for gift- or souvenir-browsing. The **Rózsavölgyi Zenebolt** (✉ V, Szervita tér 5, ☎ 1/318–3500) is an old, established music store crowded with sheet music and largely classical recordings, but with other selections as well.

Toys

For a step back into the world before Tickle Me Elmo and action figures, stop in at the tiny **Játékszerek Anno** (Toys Anno; ⊠ VI, Teréz krt. 54, ☎ 1/302–6234) store, where fabulous repros of antique European toys are sold. From simple paper puzzles to lovely stone building blocks to the 1940s wind-up metal monkeys on bicycles, these "nostalgia toys" are beautifully simple and exceptionally clever. Even if you're not a collector, it's worth a stop just to browse.

Wine

Stores specializing in Hungarian wines have become a trend in Budapest over the past few years. The best of them is the store run by the **Budapest Bortársaság** (Budapest Wine Society; ⊠ I, Batthyány u. 59, ☎ 1/212–0262, ☎ FAX 1/212–2569). The cellar shop at the base of Castle Hill always has an excellent selection of Hungary's finest wines, chosen by the wine society's discerning staff, who will happily help you with your purchases. Tastings are held Saturdays from 2 to 5 PM.

7 Side Trip: The Danube Bend

FORTY KILOMETERS NORTH of Budapest, the Danube abandons its eastward course and turns abruptly south toward the capital, cutting through the Börzsöny and Visegrád hills. This area is called the Danube Bend and includes the Baroque town of Szentendre, the hilltop castle ruins and town of Visegrád, and the cathedral town of Esztergom. The most scenically varied part of Hungary, the region is home to a chain of riverside spas and beaches, bare volcanic mountains, and limestone hills. Here, in the heartland, are the traces of the country's history—the remains of the Roman Empire's frontier, the battlefields of the Middle Ages, and the relics of the Hungarian Renaissance.

The west bank of the Danube is the more interesting side, with three charming and picturesque towns—Szentendre, Visegrád, and Esztergom. The district can be covered by car in one day, the total round-trip no more than 112 km (70 mi), although this affords only a cursory look. A day trip to Szentendre while based in Budapest plus two days for Visegrád and Esztergom, with a night in either (both have lovely small hotels), would be best.

On the Danube's eastern bank, Vác is the only larger town of any real interest. The Danube is not crossed by any bridges, but there are numerous ferries (between Visegrád and Nagymaros, Basaharc and Szob, Szentendre Island and Vác), making it possible to combine a visit to both sides of the Danube on the same excursion.

Though the Danube Bend's west bank contains the bulk of historical sights, the less-traveled east bank has the excellent hiking trails of the Börzsöny mountain range, which extends along the Danube from Vác to Zebegény before curving toward the Slovak border. The Pilis and Visegrád hills on the Danube's western side and the Börzsöny Hills on the east are popular nature escapes.

Work had started on a hydroelectric dam near Nagymaros, across from Visegrád, in the mid-1980s. The project was proposed by Austria and what was then Czechoslovakia, and reluctantly agreed to by Hungary, but protests from the Blues (Hungary's equivalent of Germany's Greens), coupled with rapid democratization, succeeded in halting the project and rescuing a region of great natural beauty. But it didn't last: The International Court at the Hague ruled in September 1998 that the original agreement between what is now Slovakia and Hungary was still valid and the two countries signed a preliminary agreement to start building the dam either at Nagymaros or Pilismarot, nearby, over the next eight years. Protests were continuing at press time.

Price categories in the dining and lodging sections in this chapter correspond to the price charts in Chapters 3 and 4.

Numbers in the margin correspond to numbers on the Danube Bend map.

Szentendre

★ ❶ *21 km (13 mi) north of Budapest.*

A romantic little town with a lively atmosphere and a flourishing artists' colony, this is the highlight of the Danube Bend. With its profusion of enchanting church steeples, colorful Baroque houses, and winding cobblestone streets, it's no wonder Szentendre attracts swarms of visitors.

Szentendre was first settled by Serbs and Greeks fleeing the advancing Turks in the 16th and 17th centuries. They built houses and churches in their own style—rich in reds and blues seldom seen elsewhere in Hungary. To truly savor Szentendre, duck into any and every cobblestone side street that appeals to you. Baroque houses with shingle roofs and colorful stone walls will enchant your eye and pique your curiosity.

Fő tér is Szentendre's picturesque main square, the centerpiece of which is an ornate **Memorial Cross** erected by Serbs in gratitude because the town was spared from a plague. The cross has a crucifixion painted on it and stands atop a triangular pillar adorned with a dozen icon paintings.

Every house on Fő tér is a designated landmark, and three of them are open to the public: the **Ferenczy Múzeum** (Ferenczy Museum) at No. 6, with paintings of Szentendre landscapes; the **Kmetty Múzeum** (Kmetty Museum) at No. 21, with works by János Kmetty, a pioneer of Hungarian avant-garde painting; and the **Szentendrei Képtár** (Municipal Gallery) at Nos. 2–5, with an excellent collection of

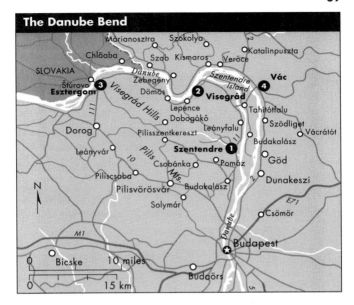

The Danube Bend

local contemporary art and international changing exhibits. ✉ *Each museum 100 Ft.* ☉ *Mid-Mar.–Oct., Tues.–Sun. 10–4; Nov.–mid-Mar., Fri.–Sun. 10–4.*

Gracing the corner of Görög utca (Greek Street) and Szentendre's main square, Fő tér, the so-called **Görög templom** (Greek Church, also known as Blagovestenska Church) is actually a Serbian Orthodox church that takes its name from the Greek inscription on a red-marble gravestone set in its wall. This elegant edifice was built between 1752 and 1754 by a rococo master, Andreas Mayerhoffer, on the site of a wooden church dating to the Great Serbian Migration (around 690). Its greatest glory—a symmetrical floor-to-ceiling panoply of stunning icons—was painted between 1802 and 1804 by Mihailo Zivkovic, a Serbian painter from Buda. ✉ *Görög u. at Fő tér.* ✉ *70 Ft.* ☉ *Mar.–Oct., Tues.–Sun. 10–5.*

If you have time for only one of Szentendre's myriad museums, don't miss the **Margit Kovács Museum,** which displays the collected works of Budapest ceramics artist Margit

Kovács, who died in 1977. She left behind a wealth of richly textured work that ranges from ceramics to life-size sculptures. Admission to the museum is limited to 15 persons at a time, so it is wise to line up early or at lunchtime, when the herds of tour groups are occupied elsewhere. ⊠ *Vastagh György u. 1 (off Görög u.)*, ☎ *26/310–244.* ✍ *250 Ft.* ☉ *Mid-Mar.–early Oct., daily 10–6; early Oct.–mid-Mar., Tues.–Sun. 10–4.*

Perched atop Vár-domb (Castle Hill) is Szentendre's oldest surviving monument, the **Katolikus plébánia templom** (Catholic Parish Church), dating to the 13th century. After many reconstructions, its oldest visible part is a 15th-century sundial in the doorway. The church's small cobblestone yard hosts an arts-and-crafts market and, often on weekends in summer, street entertainment. From here, views over Szentendre's angular tile rooftops and steeples and of the Danube beyond are superb. ⊠ *Vár-domb.* ✍ *Free.* ☉ *Erratically; check with Tourinform (*☞ *Visitor Information in Danube Bend A to Z, below).*

★   The **Szerb Ortodox Egyházi Gyüjtemény** (Serbian Orthodox Collection of Religious Art) displays exquisite artifacts relating to the history of the Serbian Orthodox Church in Hungary. Icons, altars, robes, 16th-century prayer books, and a 17th-century cross with (legend has it) a bullet hole through it were collected from all over the country, after being sold or stolen from Serbian churches that were abandoned when most Serbs returned to their homeland at the turn of the century and following World War I. The museum shares a tranquil yard with the imposing Serbian Orthodox Cathedral. ⊠ *Pátriárka u. 5*, ☎ *26/312–399.* ✍ *70 Ft.* ☉ *May–Sept., daily 10–6; Oct.–Nov. and Mar.–Apr., Tues.–Sun. 10–4; Dec.–Feb., Fri.–Sun. 10–4.*

The crimson steeple of the handsome **Szerb Ortodox Bazilika** (Serbian Orthodox Cathedral) presides over a restful tree-shaded yard crowning the hill just north of Vár-domb (Castle Hill). It was built in the 1740s with a much more lavish but arguably less beautiful iconostasis than is found in the Greek Church below it. ⊠ *Pátriárka u.*, ☎ *26/312–399.* ☉ *Erratically; check with Tourinform (*☞ *Visitor Information in Danube Bend A to Z, below) or Serbian Orthodox Collection of Religious Art museum officials.*

Dining and Lodging

$$ ★ ✕ **Aranysárkány.** On the road up to the Serbian Orthodox Cathedral, the Golden Dragon lies in wait with seven large tables, which you share with strangers on a busy night. The delicious food is prepared in a turbulent open kitchen, but all the activity is justified by the cold cherry soup with red wine or the hot *sárkány leves* (Dragon Soup) with quail eggs and vegetables. Try the grilled goose liver *Orosházi* style, wrapped in bacon and accompanied by a layered potato-and-cheese cake. The cheese dumplings with strawberry whipped cream are also recommended. ✉ *Alkotmány u. 1/a,* ☏ *26/311–670. AE, MC, V.*

$$ ★ ✕ **Rab Ráby.** Fish soup and fresh grilled trout are the specialties in this extremely popular, friendly restaurant with rustic wood beams and myriad old instruments, lanterns, cowbells, and other eclectic antiques. ✉ *Péter Pál u. 1,* ☏ *26/310–819. Reservations essential in summer. No credit cards.*

$$ ✕ **Régi Módi.** This attractive upstairs restaurant with fine wines and game specialties is approached through a courtyard across from the Margit Kovács Múzeum. Lace curtains and antique knickknacks give the small dining room a homey intimacy. The summer terrace is a delightful place to dine alfresco and look out over the red-tile rooftops. ✉ *Futó u. 3,* ☏ *26/311–105. AE, MC, V.*

$$ ✕ **Vidám Szerzetesek.** The Happy Monks opened as a family restaurant, though in recent years it has become something of a tourist haunt; the reasonably priced menu, after all, is in 20 languages. The atmosphere is casual and decidedly cheerful; the food is typically Hungarian: heavy, hearty, and delicious. Try the *Suhajda* (hat soup), topped with a tasty dough cap baked over the bowl. ✉ *Bogdányi út 3–5,* ☏ *26/310–544. AE, MC, V. Closed Mon.*

$$ **Bükkös Panzió.** Just west of the main square and across the bridge over tiny Bükkös Brook, this neat, well-run inn is one of the most conveniently located hotels in the village. The narrow staircase and small rooms give it a homey feel. ✉ *Bükkös part 16, H-2000,* ☏ *26/312–021,* ☏ FAX *26/310–782. 16 rooms. Restaurant, laundry service. MC, V.*

$$ **Kentaur Ház.** This handsome, modern, chalet-style hotel is a two-minute walk from Fő tér, on what may be Hungary's last surviving square still to bear Marx's name.

Rooms are clean and simple, with pale-gray carpeting, blond unfinished-wood paneling, and pastel-pink walls hung with original paintings by local artists. Upstairs rooms are sunniest and most spacious. ⊠ *Marx tér 3–5, H-2000,* ☎ FAX *26/312–125. 16 rooms. Bar, breakfast room. No credit cards.*

$$ ⌂ **St. Andrea Panzió.** This remodeled *panzió* atop a grassy incline has all the makings of a Swiss chalet. Attic space has been converted into modernized rooms with clean tile showers. On a warm day you can eat breakfast on the outside patio. The owners are very friendly; they've even been known to specially cook meals for guests arriving late at night. ⊠ *Egres u. 22, H-2000,* ☎ FAX *26/311–989, cellular* ☎ *06–20/230–198. 16 rooms, 2 suites. Restaurant. No credit cards.*

Nightlife and the Arts

The annual **Spring Festival,** usually held from mid-March through early April, offers classical concerts in some of Szentendre's churches, as well as jazz, folk, and rock performances in the cultural center and other venues about town. In July, the **Szentendre Summer Days** festival brings open-air theater performances and jazz and classical concerts to Fő tér and the cobblestone courtyard fronting the town hall. Although the plays are usually in Hungarian, the setting alone can make it an enjoyable experience.

Shopping

Flooded with tourists in summer, Szentendre is saturated with the requisite **souvenir shops.** Among the attractive but overpriced goods sold in every store are dolls dressed in traditional folk costumes, wooden trinkets, pottery, and colorful hand-embroidered tablecloths, doilies, and blouses. The best bargains are the hand-embroidered blankets and bags sold by dozens of elderly women in traditional folk attire, who stand for hours on the town's crowded streets.

The one tiny room of **art-éria galéria** (⊠ Városház tér 1, ☎ 26/310–111) is crammed with paintings, graphics, and sculptures by 21 of Szentendre's best contemporary artists.

Topped with an abstract-statue trio of topless, pale-pink and baby-blue women in polka-dot bikini panties, the **Christoff Galéria** (⊠ Bartók Béla u. 8, ☎ 26/317–031) is hard to miss as you climb the steep hill to its door. The gallery sells works by local and Hungarian contemporary artists, including those of ef Zambo, creator of its crowning females. It's best to call ahead to check opening times.

Beautiful stationery, booklets, and other handmade paper products are displayed and sold at the **László Vincze Paper Mill** (✉ Angyal u. 5, ☎ 26/318–501). In this small workshop at the top of a broken cobblestone street, Mr. Vincze lovingly creates his thick, watermarked paper, using traditional, 2,000-year old bleaching methods.

The sophisticated **Műhely Galéria** (✉ Fő tér 20, ☎ 26/310–139), on Szentendre's main square, displays paintings, statues, and other artworks by approximately 30 local artists.

Visegrád

❷ *23 km (14 mi) north of Szentendre.*

Visegrád was the seat of the Hungarian kings during the 14th century, when a fortress built here by the Angevin kings became the royal residence. Today, the imposing fortress at the top of the hill towers over the peaceful little town of quiet, tree-lined streets and solid old houses. The forested hills rising just behind the town offer popular hiking possibilities. For a taste of Visegrád's best, climb to the Fellegvár, and wander and take in the views of the Danube curving through the countryside; but make time to stroll around the village center a bit—on Fő utca and other streets that pique your interest.

★ Crowning a 1,148-ft hill, the dramatic **Fellegvár** (Citadel) was built in the 13th century and served as the seat of Hungarian kings in the early 14th century. In the Middle Ages, the citadel was where the Holy Crown and other royal regalia were kept, until they were stolen by a dishonorable maid of honor in 1440; 23 years later, King Matthias had to pay 80,000 Ft. to retrieve them from Austria. (Now the crown is safe in the Hungarian National Museum in Budapest.) A *panoptikum* (akin to slide projection) show portraying the era of the kings is included free with admission. The breathtaking views of the Danube Bend below are ample reward for the strenuous, 40-minute hike up. ☎ 26/

398–101. ☞ 200 Ft. ☉ Mid-Mar.–mid-Nov., daily 9–5; mid-Nov.–mid-Mar., weekends 10 AM–dusk; closed in snowy conditions.

In the 13th–14th centuries, King Matthias Corvinus had a separate palace built on the banks of the Danube below the citadel. It was eventually razed by the Turks, and not until 1934 were the ruins finally excavated. Nowadays you can see the disheveled remnants of the **Királyi palota** (Royal Palace) and its **Salamon torony** (Salomon Tower), referred to together as the **Mátyás Király Múzeum** (King Matthias Museum). The Salomon Tower houses two small exhibits displaying ancient statues and well structures from the age of King Matthiás. Especially worth seeing is the red-marble well built by a 15th-century Italian architect. Above a ceremonial courtyard rise the palace's various halls; on the left you can still see a few fine original carvings, which give an idea of how magnificent the palace must once have been. Inside the palace is a small exhibit on its history, as well as a collection of gravestones dating from Roman times to the 19th century. Fridays in May, the museum hosts medieval-crafts demonstrations. ⌧ *Fő u. 23,* ☎ *26/398-026.* ☞ *Royal Palace 250 Ft., Salomon Tower 150 Ft.* ☉ *Royal Palace: Tues.–Sun. and holidays falling on Mon. 9–4:30; Salomon Tower: May–Sept., Tues.–Sun. and holidays falling on Mon. 9–4:30.*

Dining and Lodging

$$ ✕ **Gulás Csárda.** This cozy little restaurant, decorated
★ with antique folk art and memorabilia, has only five tables inside, but additional tables are added outside during the summer. The cuisine is typical home-style Hungarian, with a limited selection of tasty traditional dishes. Try the *halászlé* (fish stew) served in a pot and kept warm on a small spirit burner. ⌧ *Nagy Lajos király u.,* ☎ *no phone. No credit cards.*

$$ ✕ **Sirály Restaurant.** Right across from the ferry station, the airy Seagull Restaurant is justifiably well regarded for its rolled fillet of venison and its many vegetarian dishes, including fried soy steak with vegetables. In summer, when cooking is often done on the terrace overlooking the Danube, expect barbecued meats and stews, soups, and *gulyas* served in old-fashioned pots. ⊠ *Rév u. 15,* ☎ *26/398–376. AE, MC, V. Closed Nov.–Feb.*

$ ✕ **Fekete Holló.** The popular "Black Raven" restaurant has an elegant yet comfortable atmosphere—a great place for a full meal or just a beer. Try the chef's creative specialties, such as coconut chicken leg with pineapples, or stick to regional staples like fresh, grilled fish; either way save room for the *palacsinta* (sweet pancakes with nuts and chocolate). ⊠ *Rév út 12,* ☎ *26/397–289. No credit cards. Closed Nov.–Mar.*

$$$ ⊡ **Silvanus.** Set high up on Fekete Hill, this hotel is renowned for its spectacular views. Rooms are bright and clean, with simple furnishings, and offer a choice of forest or Danube (1,200 Ft. more expensive) views. Since it's at the end of a steep, narrow road, the Silvanus is recommended for motorists (although a bus does stop nearby) and hikers or bikers—there are linking trails in the forest behind. ⊠ *Fekete-hegy, H-2025,* ☎ ⅢX *26/398–311 or 26/398–311. 88 rooms, 5 suites. Restaurant, bar, café, pub, bowling, mountain bikes. AE, MC, V.*

$ ⊡ **Haus Honti.** This intimate alpine-style pension is in a quiet residential area, a three-minute walk from the town center. Apple trees and a stream running close to the house create a peaceful, rustic ambience. Tiny, clean rooms are tucked under sloping ceilings and have balconies, some with lovely Danube views. Breakfast, served outdoors in nice weather, costs a couple of dollars more. ⊠ *Fő u. 66, H-2025,* ☎ *26/398–120. 7 rooms. No credit cards.*

Outdoor Activities and Sports

HIKING

Visegrád makes a great base for exploring the trails of the Visegrád and Pilis hills. A hiking map is posted on the corner of Fő utca and Rév utca, just above the pale-green Roman Catholic Parish Church. A well-trodden, well-marked hiking trail (posted with red signs) leads from the edge of Visegrád to the town of Pilisszentlászló, a wonderful 8½-km (5⅓-mi; about three-hour) journey through the oak and beech forests of the Visegrád Hills into the Pilis conservation region. Bears, bison, deer, and wild boar roam freely here and there are fields of yellow-blooming spring pheasant's eye and black pulsatilla.

SWIMMING

The outdoor thermal pools at **Lepence,** 3 km (2 mi) south-west of Visegrád on Route 11, combine good soaking with excellent Danube Bend views. ⊠ *Lepence-völgyi Termál és Strandfürdő, Lepence,* ☎ *26/398–208.* 🎫 *350 Ft.* ☉ *Daily May–Sept. 9–6:30*

Esztergom

❸ *21 km (13 mi) north of Visegrád.*

Esztergom stands on the site of a Roman fortress, at the westernmost curve of the heart-shape Danube Bend, where the Danube marks the border between Hungary and Slovakia. (The bridge that once joined these two countries was destroyed by the Nazis near the end of World War II, though parts of the span can still be seen.) St. Stephen, the first Christian king of Hungary and founder of the nation, was crowned here in the year 1000, establishing Esztergom as Hungary's first capital, which it remained for the next 250 years. The majestic Bazilika, Hungary's largest, is Esztergom's main draw, followed by the fine art collection of the Primate's Palace. If you like strolling, leave yourself a little time to explore the narrow streets of Viziváros (Watertown) below the Bazilika, lined with brightly painted Baroque buildings.

★ Esztergom's **Bazilika** (cathedral), the largest in Hungary, stands on a hill overlooking the town; it is now the seat of the cardinal primate of Hungary. It was here, in the center of Hungarian Catholicism, that the famous anti-Communist cleric, Cardinal József Mindszenty, was finally reburied in 1991, ending an era of religious intolerance and prosecution and a sorrowful chapter in Hungarian history. Its most interesting features are the Bakócz Chapel (1506), named for a primate of Hungary who only narrowly missed becoming pope; and the sacristy, which contains a valuable collection of medieval ecclesiastical art. If your timing is lucky, you could attend a concert during one of the various classical music festivals held here in summer (☞ Nightlife and the Arts, *below*). ⊠ *Szent István tér,* ☎ *33/311–895.* 🎫 *Free.* ☉ *Apr.–late Oct., daily 7–6; late Oct.–Mar., weekdays 7–4, weekends 7–5.*

Considered by many to be Hungary's finest art gallery, the **Keresztény Múzeum** (Museum of Christian Art), in the Primate's Palace, has a thorough collection of early Hungarian and Italian paintings (the 14th- and 15th-century Italian collection is unusually large for a museum outside Italy). Unique holdings include the *Coffin of Our Lord* from Garamszentbenedek; the wooden statues of the Apostles and of the Roman soldiers guarding the coffin are masterpieces of Hungarian Baroque sculpture. The building also holds the Primate's Archives, which contain 20,000 volumes, including several medieval codices. Permission to visit the archives must be obtained in advance. *Primate's Palace:* ⊠ *Mindszenty tér 2,* ☎ *33/413–880.* ☎ *150 Ft.* ☉ *Mid-Mar.–Sept., Tues.–Sun. 10–6; Oct.–Dec. and first 2 wks of Mar., Tues.–Sun. 10–5.*

To the south of the cathedral, on **Szent Tamás Hill,** is a small church dedicated to St. Thomas à Becket of Canterbury. From here you can look down on the town and see how the Danube temporarily splits, forming an island, **Prímás-sziget,** that locals use as a base for waterskiing and swimming, in spite of the pollution. To reach it, cross the Kossuth Bridge.

Dining and Lodging

$$ ✗ **Kispipa.** Lively and not far from the town center, this place is especially memorable for its good choice of wines. The food menu includes soups, stews, and traditional Hungarian dishes such as fried goose with heavy cream. ⊠ *Kossuth Lajos utca 19,* ☎ *no phone. Reservations not accepted. No credit cards.*

$$ ✗ **Prímáspince.** Arched ceilings and exposed brick walls make a charming setting for refined Hungarian fare at this touristy but good restaurant just below the cathedral. Try the tournedos Budapest style (tender beef with sautéed vegetables and paprika) or the thick turkey breast Fiaker style (stuffed with ham and melted cheese). ⊠ *Szent István tér 4,* ☎ *33/313–495. AE, DC, MC, V. No dinner Jan.–Feb.*

$$ 🏨 **Alabárdos Panzió.** Conveniently located downhill from the cathedral, this cozy, remodeled home provides excellent views from upstairs. Rooms (doubles and quads) are small but less cramped than at other small pensions. ⊠ *Baj-*

csy-Zsilinszky u. 49, H-2500, ☎ FAX *33/312–640. 21 rooms. Breakfast room. No credit cards.*

$$ 🏨 **Hotel Esztergom.** Simply furnished and sports-oriented, this hotel has a good location on Primás-sziget. Tennis, swimming, bowling, horseback riding, and watersports facilities are nearby. All rooms have balconies. ⊠ *Primás sziget, Nagy Duna Sétány, H-2500,* ☎ *33/312–883,* FAX *33/312–853. 34 rooms, 2 suites. Restaurant, bar, café, meeting room. AE, MC, V.*

Nightlife and the Arts

Every two years Esztergom hosts the **Nemzetközi Gitár Fesztivál** (International Guitar Festival) during which renowned classical guitarists from around the world hold master classes and workshops for participants. Recitals are held nearly every night in Esztergom's **Zöldház Művelődési Központ** (Green House Cultural Center) or the **Tanítóképzőiskola** (Teaching University), where the festival is based, or elsewhere in Budapest and neighboring towns. The climax of it all is the glorious closing concert, held in the basilica, in which the hundreds of participants join together and perform as a guitar orchestra. The festival runs for two weeks, usually beginning in early August; the next one will be held in 1999. Tickets and information are available at the tourist offices.

Vác

❹ *34 km (21 mi) north of Budapest; 20 km (12 mi) south of Nagymaros, which is accessed by ferry from Visegrád.*

With its lovely riverfront promenade, its cathedral, and less delightful Triumphal Arch, the small city of Vác, on the Danube's east bank, is well worth a short visit if only to watch the sun slowly set from the promenade. Vác's historic town center is full of pretty Baroque buildings in matte yellows and reds and offers many visual rewards and photo opportunities for those who wander onto a few of its narrow cobblestone side streets heading in toward the river.

Vác's 18th-century **Székesegyház** (cathedral) on Konstantin tér is an outstanding example of Hungarian neoclassicism. It was built in 1763–1777 by Archbishop Kristóf Migazzi to the designs of the Italian architect Isidor

Carnevale; the most interesting features are the murals by the Austrian Franz Anton Maulbertsch, both on the dome and behind the altar. Exquisite frescoes decorate the walls inside. ⊠ *Konstantin tér,* ☎ *27/317–010.* 🖼 *20 Ft.* ☉ *Apr.– Sept. (weather permitting), daily 9–6; Oct.–Mar. with advance arrangements only.*

In 1764, when Archbishop Migazzi heard that Queen Maria Theresa planned to visit his humble town, he hurriedly arranged the construction of a **triumphal arch.** The queen came and left, but the awkward arch remains, at the edge of the city's historic core next to a cement-and-barbed-wire prison complex. ⊠ *Köztársaság út, just past Barabás utca.*

The **promenade** along the Danube is a wonderful place to stroll or picnic, looking out at the flashing river or back toward the pretty, historic town. The main entrance to the riverfront area is from Petróczy utca, which begins at the cathedral on Konstantin tér and feeds straight into the promenade.

Vácrátóti Arborétum, 4 km (2½ mi) from Vác, is Hungary's biggest and best botanical garden, with more than 12,000 plant species. The arboretum's top priority is botanical research and collection under the auspices of the Hungarian Academy of Sciences, but you're welcome to stroll along the paths and sit on benches in the leafy shade. If you're driving from Vác, follow signs towards Gödöllő, then towards Vácrátót. ⊠ *Alkotmány u. 4–6,* ☎ *28/360–122 or 28/360–147.* 🖼 *120 Ft.* ☉ *Apr.–Sept., daily 8–6; Oct.– Mar., daily 8–4.*

Dining

$ ✕ **Halászkert Étterem.** The large terrace of this riverfront restaurant next to the ferry landing is a popular place for a hearty lunch or dinner of Hungarian fish specialties. ⊠ *Liszt Ferenc sétány 9,* ☎ *27/315–985. AE, MC, V.*

Nightlife and the Arts

In July and August, a series of outdoor classical concerts is held in the verdant **Vácrátóti Arborétum** (☞ *above*). The last weekend in July brings the **Váci Világi Vigalom** (Vác World Jamboree) festival, with folk dancing, music, crafts fairs, and other festivities throughout town.

Outdoor Activities and Sports

Vác is the gateway to hiking in the forests of the **Börzsöny Hills,** rich in natural springs, castle ruins, and splendid Danube Bend vistas. Consult the Börzsöny hiking map, available at Tourinform, for planning a walk on the well-marked trails. The **Börzsöny Természetjáró Kör** (Börzsöny Nature Walk Group) organizes free guided nature walks every other Sunday all year round. Naturally, Hungarian is the official language, but chances are good that younger group members will speak English—but even without understanding what is spoken, the trips afford a nice opportunity to be guided through the area. Contact Tourinform (☞ Visitor Information *in* Danube Bend A to Z, *below*) for details.

Danube Bend A to Z

Arriving and Departing

BY BOAT

If you have enough time, you can travel to the west-bank towns by boat from Budapest, a leisurely and pleasant journey, especially in summer and spring. Boating from Budapest to Esztergom takes about five hours, to Visegrád about three hours. Boats leave from the main Pest dock at Vigadó tér. The disadvantage of boat travel is that a round-trip by slow boat doesn't allow much time for sightseeing; the Esztergom route, for example, allows only under two hours before it's time to head back. Many people head upriver by boat in the morning and back down by bus or train as it's getting dark. There is daily service from Budapest to Visegrád, stopping in Szentendre. Less frequent boats go to Vác, on the east bank, as well. Contact **MAHART** in Budapest for complete schedule information (☎ 1/318–1704).

BY BUS

Buses run regularly between Budapest's Árpád híd bus station and most towns along both sides of the Danube. The ride to Szentendre is about half an hour.

BY CAR

Route 11 runs along the western shore of the Danube, connecting Budapest to Szentendre, Visegrád, and Esztergom. Route 2 runs along the eastern shore for driving between Budapest and Vác.

Vác and Esztergom have frequent daily express and local train service to and from Budapest's Nyugati (Western) Station. Trains do not run to Visegrád. The **HÉV** suburban railway runs between Batthyány tér (or Margaret Island, one stop north) in Budapest and Szentendre about every 10 to 20 minutes every day; the trip takes 40 minutes and costs around 180 Ft.

Getting Around
BY BOAT
Boat travel along the river is slow and scenic. **MAHART**'s (☞ Arriving and Departing, *above*) boats ply the river between Budapest and Esztergom, Szentendre, and Visegrád. You can plan your sightseeing to catch a boat connection from one town to the other (☞ Arriving and Departing, *above*).

BY BUS
Buses are cheap and relatively comfortable; they link all major towns along both banks. If you don't have a car, this is the best way to get around, since train service is spotty.

BY FERRY
As there are no bridges across the Danube in this region, there is regular daily passenger and car **ferry service** between several points on opposite sides of the Danube (except in winter when the river is too icy). The crossing generally takes about 10 minutes and costs roughly 400 Ft. per car and about 100 Ft. per passenger. The crossing between Nagymaros and Visegrád is recommended, as it affords gorgeous views of Visegrád's citadel and includes a beautiful drive through rolling hills on Route 12 south of Nagymaros. Contact the relevant tourist office (☞ Visitor Information, *below*) for schedule details.

Contacts and Resources
GUIDED TOURS
IBUSZ Travel (☎ 1/319–7520 or 1/319–7519) organizes daylong bus trips from Budapest along the Danube, stopping in Esztergom, Visegrád, and Szentendre on Tuesdays, Fridays, and Sundays from May through October, and Saturdays only from November through April. There's commentary in English; the cost, including lunch and admission fees, is about 13,000 Ft.

Gray Line Cityrama (in Budapest, ☏ 1/302–4382) runs its popular "Danube Tour" (approximately 13,000 Ft.) daily Wednesday–Sunday from May until September. The full day begins with sightseeing in Visegrád, then Esztergom. After lunch, the tour moves on to Szentendre for a guided walk and makes a scenic return to Budapest down the Danube. (The tour returns by bus when the water level is low and in winter, when the tour is offered once a week.)

VISITOR INFORMATION

Budapest: Tourinform (⊠ V, Sütő u. 2, ☏ 1/317–9800). **Esztergom:** Grantours (⊠ Széchenyi tér 25, ☏ FAX 33/413–756); IBUSZ (⊠ Kossuth L. u. 5, ☏ 33/312–552); Komtourist (⊠ Lőrinc u. 6, ☏ 33/312–082). **Szentendre:** Tourinform (⊠ Dumsta J. u. 22, ☏ FAX 26/317–965). **Vác:** Tourinform (⊠ Dr. Csányi krt. 45, ☏ 27/316–160). **Visegrád:** Visegrád Tours (⊠ Sirály Restaurant, Rév u. 15, ☏ FAX 26/398–160).

HUNGARIAN VOCABULARY

English	Hungarian	Pronunciation

Common Greetings

English	Hungarian	Pronunciation
Hello (good day).	Jó napot./Jó napot kivánok.	**yoh** nuh-poht/**yoh** nuh-poht **kee**-vah-nohk
Good-bye.	Viszontlátásra.	**vee**-sohnt-lah-tahsh-ruh
Hello/Good-bye (informal).	Szervusz.	**ser**-voos
Good morning.	Jó reggelt kivánok.	**yoh** reg-gelt **kee**-vah-nohk
Good evening.	Jó estét kivánok.	**yoh** esh-tayt **kee**-vah-nohk
Ma'am	Asszonyom	**uhs**-sohn-yohm
Miss	Kisasszony	**keesh**-uhs-sohny
Mr./Sir	Uram	**oor**-uhm

To address someone as Mrs., add the suffix "né" to the last name. Mrs. Kovács is then "Kovácsné." To address someone as Mr., use the word "úr" after the last name. Mr. Kovács is then "Kovács úr."

English	Hungarian	Pronunciation
Good morning, Mrs. Kovács/ Mr. Kovács	Jó reggelt, Kovácsné/ Kovács úr.	**yoh** reg-gelt **koh**-vahch-nay/ **koh**-vahch oor
How are you?	Hogy van?	**hohdge** vuhn
Fine, thanks. And you?	Jól vagyok, köszönöm. És maga?	**yohl** vuhdge-ohk **ku(r)**-su(r)-nu(r)m aysh **muh**-guh
What is your name?	Hogy hívják?	**hohdge heev**-yahk
What is your name (informal)?	Hogy hívnak?	**hohdge** heev-nuhk
My name is . . .	(Name) vagyok.	**vuhdge**-ohk
Good luck!	Jó szerencsét!	**yoh se**-ren-chayt

This material is adapted from Living Language™ *Fast & Easy* Hungarian (Crown Publishers, Inc.). *Fast & Easy "survival" courses are available in 15 different languages, including Czech, Hungarian, Polish, and Russian. Each interactive 60-minute cassette teaches more than 300 essential phrases for travelers. Available in bookstores or call 800/733–3000 to order.*

Polite Expressions

Please	Kérem szépen	**kay**-rem **say**-pen
Thank you.	Köszönöm.	**ku(r)**-su(r)-nu(r)m
Thank you very much.	Nagyon szépen köszönöm.	**nuhdge**-ohn **say**-pen **ku(r)**-su(r)-nu(r)m
You're welcome.	Kérem szépen.	**kay**-rem **say**-pen
You're welcome (informal).	Szivesen.	**see**-vesh-en
Yes, thank you.	Igen, köszönöm.	**ee**-gen **ku(r)**-su(r)-nu(r)m
No, thank you.	Nem, köszönöm.	**nem ku(r)**-su(r)-nu(r)m
Pardon me.	Bocsánat./Elnézést kerek.	**boh**-chah-nuht/**el**-nay-zaysht **kay**-rek
I'm sorry (sympathy, regret).	Sajnálom.	**shuhy**-nahl-ohm
I don't understand.	Nem értem.	nem **ayr**-tem
I don't speak Hungarian very well.	Nem beszélek jól magyarul.	nem **bess**-ayl-ek yohl **muh**-dgeuhr-ool
Do you speak English?	Beszél angolul?	**be**-sayl **uhn**-gohl-ool
Yes/No	Igen/Nem	**ee**-gen/nem
Speak slowly, please.	Kérem, beszéljen lassan.	**kay**-rem **bess**-ay-yen **luhsh**-shuhn
Repeat, please.	Ismételje meg, kérem.	**eesh**-may-tel-ye meg **kay**-rem
I don't know.	Nem tudom.	**nem** too-dohm
Here you are (when giving something).	Tessék.	**tesh**-shayk
Excuse me (what did you say)?	Tessék?	**tesh**-shayk

Questions

What is . . . What is this?	Mi . . . Mi ez?	**mee** ez
When . . . When will they be ready?	Mikor . . . Mikor lesznek készen?	**mee**-kor **less**-nek **kayss**-en
Why . . . Why is the pastry shop closed?	Miért . . . Miért van zárva a cukrászda?	**mee**-ayrt vuhn **zahr**-vuh uh **tsook**-rahss-duh

Who . . . Who is your friend?	Ki . . . Ki a barátod?	**kee** uh **buh**-raht-ohd
How . . . How do you say this in Hungarian?	Hogy . . . Hogy mondják ezt magyarul?	**hohdge mohnd**-yahk ezt **muh**-dgeuhr-ool
Which . . . Which train goes to Esztergom?	Melyik . . . Melyik vonat megy Esztergomba?	**mey**-eek **voh**-nuht **medge ess**-ter-gohm-buh
What do you want to do?	Mit akar csinálni?	**meet** uh-kuhr **chee**-nahl-nee
What do you want to do (informal)?	Mit akarsz csinálni?	**meet** uh-kuhrss **chee**-nahl-nee
Where are you going?	Hova megy?	**hoh**-vuh medge
Where are you going (informal)?	Hova mész?	**hoh**-vuh mayss
What is the date today?	Hanyadika van ma?	**huh**-nyuh-deek-uh vuhn muh
May I?	Szabad?	**suh**-buhd
May I take this?	Szabad ezt elven-ni?	**suh**-buhd ezt **el**-ven-nee

Directions

Where	Hol	hohl
Excuse me, where is the . . . ?	Elnézést, hol van a . . . ?	**el**-nay-zaysht **hohl** vuhn uh
Excuse me, where is Castle Hill?	Elnézést, hol van a vár?	**el**-nay-zaysht **hohl** vuhn uh **vahr**
Where is the toilet?	Hol van a WC?	**hohl** vuhn uh **vay**-tsay
Where is the bus stop?	Hol van a buszmegálló?	**hohl** vuhn uh **booss**-meg-ahl-loh
Where is the subway station?	Hol van a metró?	**hohl** vuhn uh **met**-roh
Go	Menjen	**men**-yen
To the right	Jobbra	**yohb**-bruh
To the left	Balra	**buhl**-ruh
Straight ahead	Egyenessen előre	**edge**-en-esh-shen **e**-lu(r)-re
At the end of the street	Az utca végén	uhz **oot**-suh **vay**-gayn
The first left	Az első balra	uhz **el**-shu(r) **buhl**-ruh
Near	Közel	**ku(r)z**-el
It's near here.	Közel van ide.	**ku(r)z**-el vuhn **ee**-de

Turn	Forduljon	**fohr**-dool-yohn
Go back.	Menjen vissza.	**men**-yen **vees**-suh
Next to . . .	. . . mellett	. . . **mel**-lett

At the Hotel

Room	Szoba	**soh**-buh
I would like a room.	Kérek egy szobát.	**kay**-rek edge **soh**-baht
For one person	Egy személyre	**edge sem**-ay-re
For two people	Két személyre	**kayt sem**-ay-re
For how many nights?	Hány éjszakára?	**hahny**-suhk-ah-ruh
For tonight	Ma éjszakára	**muh ay**-suhk-ah-ruh
For two nights	Két éjszakára	**kayt ay**-suhk-ah-ruh
For a week	Egy hétre	**edge hayt**-re
Do you have a different room?	Van egy másik szoba?	vuhn edge **mahsh**-eek **soh**-buh
With a bath	Fürdőszobával	**fewr**-du(r)-soh-bah-vuhl
With a shower	Zuhanyal	**zoo**-huhn-yuhl
With a toilet	WC-vel	**vay**-tsay vel
The key, please.	Kérem a kulcsot.	**kay**-rem uh **koolch**-oht
How much is it?	Mennyibe kerül?	**men**-yee-be **ker**-ewl
My bill, please.	Kérem a számlát.	**kay**-rem uh **sahm**-laht

At the Restaurant

Café	Kávéház	**kah**-vay-hahz
Restaurant	Étterem	**ayt**-ter-rem
Where is a good restaurant?	Hol van egy jó étterem?	hohl vuhn edge **yoh ayt**-ter-rem
Reservation	Rezerváció	**re**-zer-vah-tsee-oh
Table for two	Asztal két személyre	**uhss**-tuhl kayt **sem**-ay-re
Waiter	Pincér	**peen**-sayr
Waitress	Pincérnő	**peen**-sayr-nu(r)

(Waiters and waitresses are more likely to respond to the request "Legyen szíves" [**ledge**-en-see-vesh], which means "please.")

| I would like the menu, please. | Kérem az étlapot. | **kay**-rem uhz **ayt**-luhp-oht |

The wine list, please.	Kérem a borlapot.	**kay**-rem uh **bohr**-luhp oht
Appetizers	Előételek	**el**-u(r)-ay-tel-ek
Main course	Főétel	**fu(r)**-ay-tel
Dessert	Deszert	**dess**-ert
What would you like to drink?	Mit tetszik inni?	meet **tet**-seek **een**-nee
A beer, please.	Egy sört kérek.	edge shurt **kay**-rek
Wine, please.	Bort kérek.	**bohrt kay**-rek
The specialty of the day	A mai ajánlat	uh **muh**-ee **uhy**-ahn-luht
What would you like?	Mit tetszik parancsolni?	meet **tet**-seek **puh**-ruhn-chohl-nee
Can you recommend a good wine?	Tudna ajánlani egy finom bort?	**tood**-nuh **uhy**-ahn-luhn-ee edge **fee**-nohm bohrt
I didn't order this.	Ezt nem rendeltem.	ezt **nem ren**-del-tem
The check, please.	Kérem szépen a számlát.	**kay**-rem **say**-pen uh **sahm**-laht
Is the tip included?	Benne van a borravallo?	**ben**-ne vuhn uh **bohr**-ruh-vuhl-loh
Breakfast	Reggeli	**reg**-gel-ee
Lunch	Ebéd	**e**-bayd
Supper	Vacsora	**vuh**-chohr-uh
Bon appetit.	Jó étvágyat.	**yoh ayt**-vahdge-uht
To your health!	Egészségére!	**e**-gayss-shayg-ay-re
Fork	Villa	**veel**-luh
Knife	Kés	kaysh
Spoon	Kanál	**kuh**-nahl
Napkin	Szalvéta	**suhl**-vay-tuh
Cup of tea	Téa	**tay**-uh
Bottle of wine	Üveg bor	**ew**-veg **bohr**
Ice	Jég	yayg
Salt and pepper	Só és bors	shoh aysh bohrsh
Sugar	Cukor	**tsoo**-kohr
Soup	Leves	**le**-vesh
Salad	Saláta	**shuhl**-ah-tuh
Vegetables	Zöldség	**zu(r)ld**-shayg
Beef	Marhahús	**muhr**-huh-hoosh
Chicken	Csirke	**cheer**-ke
Bread	Kenyér	**ken**-yayr
Black coffee	Fekete kávé	**fe**-ke-te **kah**-vay

Coffee with milk	Tejeskávé	**tey**-esh-**kah**-vay
Tea with lemon	Téa citrommal	**tey**-uh **tseet**-rohm-muhl
Orange juice	Narancslé	**nuh**-ruhnch-lay
Mineral water	Ásványvíz	**ahsh**-vahn'y-veez
Another	Még egy	**mayg** edge
I'd like some more mineral water.	Kérek még egy ásványvízet.	**kay**-rek **meyg** edge **ahsh**-vahny-veez-et
I'd like some more bread and butter.	Kérek még kenyeret és vajat.	**kay**-rek mayg **ken**-yer-et aysh **vuhy**-uht
Is it very spicy?	Nagyon csípős ez?	**nuhdge**-ohn **chee**-pu(r)sh ez
May I exchange this?	Ezt kicserélhetem?	ezt **kee**-che-rayl-het-em

Numbers

0	Nulla	**nool**-luh
1	Egy	edge
2	Kettő	**ket**-tu(r)
3	Három	**hah**-rohm
4	Négy	naydge
5	Öt	u(r)t
6	Hat	huht
7	Hét	hayt
8	Nyolc	nyohlts
9	Kilenc	**kee**-lents
10	Tíz	teez
11	Tizenegy	**teez**-en-edge
12	Tizenkettő	**teez**en-ket-tu(r)
13	Tizenhárom	**teez**-en-hah-rohm
14	Tizennégy	**teez**-en-naydge
15	Tizenöt	**teez**-en-u(r)t
16	Tizenhat	**teez**-en-huht
17	Tizenhét	**teez**-en-hayt
18	Tizennyolc	**teez**-en-nyohlts
19	Tizenkilenc	**teez**-en-kee-lents
20	Húsz	hooss
21	Huszonegy	**hooss**-ohn-edge
22	Huszonkettő	**hooss**-ohn-ket-tu(r)
30	Harminc	**huhr**-meents
40	Negyven	**nedge**-ven
50	Ötven	**u(r)t**-ven
60	Hatvan	**huht**-vuhn

70	Hetven	**het**-ven
80	Nyolcvan	**nyohlts**-vuhn
90	Kilencven	**kee**-lents-ven
100	Száz	sahz
1,000	Ezer	**e**-zer

Telling Time

What time is it?	Hány óra van?	**hahny oh**-ruh vuhn
Midnight	Éjfél	**ay**-fayl
It is 9:00 AM.	Reggel kilenc óra van.	**reg**-gel **kee**-lents **oh**-ruh vuhn
10:00 AM	Reggel tíz óra	**reg**-gel **teez oh**-ruh
It is noon.	Dél van.	**dayl** vuhn
It is 1:00 PM.	Délután egy óra van.	**dayl**-oo-tahn **edge oh**-ruh vuhn
It is 6:00 PM.	Délután hat óra van.	**dayl**-oo-tahn **huht oh**-ruh vuhn
Minute	Perc	perts
3:20 PM	Délután három óra húsz perc	**dayl**-oo-tahn **hah**-rohm **oh**-ruh hooss perts
8:30 AM	Reggel nyolc óra harminc perc	**reg**-gel **nyohlts oh**-ruh **huhr**-meents perts
Early morning	Hajnal	**huhy**-nuhl
Morning	Reggel	**reg**-gel
Before noon	Délelőtt	**dayl**-el-u(r)t
Afternoon	Délután	**dayl**-oo-tahn
Evening	Este	**esh**-te
Night	Éjszaka	**ay**-suhk-uh
Now	Most	mohsht
Later	Később	**kay**-shu(r)b
Immediately	Mindjárt	**meen**-dyahrt
Soon	Hamarossan	**huh**-muh-rohsh-shuhn

Days of the Week

Monday	Hétfő	**hayt**-fu(r)
Tuesday	Kedd	ked
Wednesday	Szerda	**ser**-duh
Thursday	Csütörtök	**chew**-tur-tu(r)k
Friday	Péntek	**payn**-tek
Saturday	Szombat	**sohm**-buht
Sunday	Vasárnap	**vuh**-shahr-nuhp

Months

English	Hungarian	Pronunciation
January	Január	**yuh**-noo-ahr
February	Február	**feb**-roo-ahr
March	Március	**mahr**-tsee-oosh
April	Április	**ah**-pree-leesh
May	Május	**mah**-yoosh
June	Június	**yoo**-nee-oosh
July	Július	**yoo**-lee-oosh
August	Augusztus	**ow**-goost-oosh
September	Szeptember	**sep**-tem-ber
October	Október	**ohk**-toh-ber
November	November	**noh**-vem-ber
December	December	**de**-tsem-ber

Shopping

English	Hungarian	Pronunciation
Money	Pénz	paynz
Where is the bank?	Hol van a bank?	hohl vohn uh **buhnk**
I would like to change some money.	Szeretnék pénzt beváltani.	**Se**-ret-nayk paynzt **be**-vahl-tuh-nee
Please write it down.	Kérem írja fel.	**kay**-rem **eer**-yuh fel
How can I help you?	Tessék parancsolni?	**tesh**-shayk **puh**-ruhn-chohl-nee
I would like this.	Ezt kérem.	ezt **kay**-rem
Here it is.	Tessék itt van.	**tesh**-shayk eet vuhn
Would you care for anything else?	Más valamit?	**mahsh** **vuh**-luh-meet
That's all, thanks.	Mást nem kérek, köszönöm.	mahsht nem **kay**-rek **ku(r)**-su(r)-nu(r)m
Would you accept a traveler's check?	Elfogadják az utazási csekket?	**el**-foh-guhd-yahk uhz **oot**-uhz-ahsh-ee **chek**-ket
Credit card?	Hitelkártya?	**hee**-tel-kahr-tyuh
How much?	Mennyi?	**men**-nyee
Department store	Áruház	**ah**-roo-hahz
Bakery	Pékség	**payk**-shayg
Pastry shop	Cukrászda	**tsook**-rahz-duh
Grocery store	Élelmiszerbolt	**ayl**-el-mees-er-bohlt
Butcher's shop	Hentes	**hen**-tesh

I would like a loaf of bread.	Kérek egy kenyeret.	**kay**-rek edge **ke**-nyer-et
Bottle of white wine	Üveg fehérbor	**ew**-veg **fe**-hayr-bohr
I would like 30 dekagrams of cheese.	Kérek harminc deka sajtot.	**kay**-rek **huhr**-meents **de**-kuh **shuhy**-toht
Give me six apples.	Tessék adni hat almát.	**tesh**-shayk **uhd**-nee **huht uhl**-maht
Clothing	Ruha	**roo**-huh
Woman's clothing	Nőiruha	**nu(r)**-ee-roo-huh
Toys and gifts	Játék és ajándék	**yah**-tayk aysh **uh**-yahn-dayk
Folk art and embroideries	Népművészet és kézimunka	**nayp**-mew-vays-et aysh **kay**-zee-moon-kuh

The Post Office

Post office	Posta	**pohsh**-tuh
Where is the post office?	Hol van a posta?	**hohl** vuhn uh **pohsh**-tuh
Some stamps, please.	Bélyegeket kérek.	**bay**-yeg-ek-et **kay**-rek
For letters or postcards?	Levélre vagy képeslapra?	**le**-vayl-re vuhdge **kay**-pesh-luhp-ruh
Where are you sending them?	Hova küldi?	**hoh**-vuh **kewl**-dee
To the United States	Az Egyesült Államokba	uhz **edge**-esh-ewlt **ahl**-luhm-ohk-buh
Airmail	Légiposta	**lay**-gee-pohsh-tuh
Telephone directory	Telefonkönyv	**te**-le-fohn-ku(r)nyv
Where can I telephone?	Hol lehet telefonálni?	hohl **le**-het **te**-le-fohn-ahl-nee
Telephone call	Telefonhívás	**te**-le-fohn-heev-ahsh
What number, please?	Melyik telefonszámat kéri?	**me**-yeek **te**-le-fohn-sahm-uht **kay**-ree
The line is busy.	Foglalt a vonal.	**fohg**-luhlt uh **voh**-nuhl
There's no answer, try again later.	Nincs válasz, tessék később próbálni.	**neench vah**-luhs **tesh**-shayk **kay**-shu(r)b **proh**-bahl-nee
May I speak to . . . ?	Beszélhetek . . . ?	**be**-sayl-he-tek

| May I leave a message? | Hagyhatok üzenetet? | **huhdge**-huh-tohk **ew**-ze-net-et |

The Airport

Where is customs?	Hol van a vám?	hohl vuhn uh **vahm**
Where is the passport control?	Hol van az útlevélellenőrzés?	hohl vuhn uhz **oot**-le-vayl-**el**-len-ur-zaysh
Where does the baggage arrive?	Hol érkeznek a csomagok?	hohl **ayr**-kez-nek uh **choh**-muhg-ohk
Where is the departures wing?	Hol van az indulási oldal?	hohl vuhn uhz **een**-dool-ahsh-ee **ohl**-duhl
Where is the arrivals wing?	Hol van az érkezési oldal?	hohl vuhn uhz **ayr**-kez-ay-shee **ohl**-duhl
Where is a taxi?	Hol van a taxi?	hohl vuhn uh **tuhx**-ee
Where is the exit?	Hol van a kijárat?	hohl vuhn uh **kee**-yahr-uht
Is there a subway or a bus here?	Van itt metró vagy autóbusz?	vuhn eet **met**-roh vuhdy **ow**-toh-boos
Stop here, please.	Kérem szépen, álljon meg itt.	**kay**-rem **say**-pen **ahl**-yohn meg eet
What is the fare to the Parliament?	Mennyi az ár a Parlementig?	**men**-yee uhz ahr uh **puhr**-le-men-teeg
What is the fare?	Mennyi a viteldíj?	**men**-yee uh **vee**-tel-dee

The Train Station

I would like a ticket, please.	Egy jegyet kérek.	edge **yedge**-et **kay**-rek
A return ticket	Egy retur jegy	edge **re**-toor yedge
First class	Első osztályú	**el**-shu(r) **ohs**-tahy-oo
Do you have a timetable?	Van itt menetrend?	vuhn eet **me**-net-rend
Is there a dining car?	Van étkezőkocsi?	vuhn **ayt**-kez-u(r)-koh-chee
Sleeping car	Hálókocsi	**hah**-loh-koh-chee
Where is this train going?	Hova megy ez a vonat?	**hoh**-vuh medge ez uh **voh**-nuht
When does the train leave for Pécs?	Mikor indul a vonat Pécsre?	**mee**-kohr **een**-dool uh **voh**-nuht **paych**-re

When does the train arrive from Pécs?	Mikor érkezik a vonat Pécsröl?	**mee**-kohr **ayr**-kez-eek uh **voh**-nuht **paych**-ru(r)l
The train is late.	A vonat késik.	uh **voh**-nuht **kay**-sheek
Can you help me, please?	Tudna segíteni?	**tood**-nuh **she**-geet-e-nee
Can you tell me . . . ?	Meg tudna mondani . . . ?	**meg** tood-nuh **mohn**-duh-nee
I've lost my bags.	Elvesztettem a csomagjaimat.	**el**-ves-tet-tem uh **choh**-muhg-yuh-ee-muht

MENU GUIDE

Getting Started

waiter/waitress	pincér/pincérnő
menu	étlap
wine list	borlap
beverage list	itallap
without meat	hústalan
breakfast	reggeli
lunch	ebéd
supper	vacsora
cup/saucer	csésze/tányér
appetizers	előetelek
soups	levesek
salads	saláták
vegetables	köretek
fish	halak
poultry	szárnyas
game	vadas
meat	hús
dessert	deszert
sweets	édességek
fruit	gyümölcs
beverages	italok

Breakfast

bread	kenyér
roll	zsemle
butter	vaj
jam/jelly	lekvár
warm/hot	meleg/forró
cold	hideg
milk	tej
fruit juice	gyümölcslé
eggs	tojások
hard-boiled egg	keménytojás
soft-boiled egg	lágytojás
scrambled eggs	rántotta
ham	sonka
bacon	szalonna
lemon	citrom
sugar	cukor

Appetizers, Snacks, Side Dishes

fruit salad	gyümölcs saláta
cucumber salad	uborka saláta
cheese	sajt
potatoes	burgonya
french fries	sült krumpli
rice	rízs
red cabbage	vöröskáposzta
sandwich	szendvics
Hungarian salami	téliszalami
sausage	kolbasz
frankfurter	vírsli
Hungarian biscuits	pogácsa
fried dough	lángos
cheese-filled Hungarian crepes	túróspalacsinta

Soups

bean soup	bableves
goulash soup (beef stew)	gulyásleves
cold cherry soup	meggyleves
fish stew with paprika	halászlé

Vegetables

cauliflower	karfiol
string beans	zöldbabfőzelék
potatoes	krumpli
onion	hagyma
spinach	spenót
mushroom	gomba
cabbage	káposzta
corn	kukorica
cucumber	uborka
tomato	paradicsom
stuffed cabbage	töltöttkáposzta
potato casserole	rakottkrumpli

Fish

carp	ponty
local fish	fogas
catfish	harcsa

Poultry

chicken	csirke
turkey	pulyka

duck   kacsa
goose   liba
goose liver   libamáj

Meat
veal   borjú
beef   marhahús
lamb   bárány
ham   sonka
pork   sertéshús
breaded meat   rántotthús
chicken paprika   paprikáscsirke
steak   rostélyos

Desserts, Fruit
sweets   édesség
ice cream   fagylalt
whipped cream   tejszínhab
cake   torta
Hungarian crepes   palacsinta
strudel   rétes
chestnut cream   gesztenyecrém
chocolate   csokoládé
walnuts   dió
apple   alma
orange   narancs
pear   körte
sour cherries   meggy
apricot   barack
melon   dinye
layer cake with hardened,   dobostorta
caramelized top

Beverages
bottle   üveg
glass   pohár
cup   csésze
beer   sör
wine   bor
white wine   fehér bor
red wine   vörös bor
brandy   pálinka
apricot brandy   barackpálinka
vodka   vodka

lemonade	limonadé
water	víz
mineral water	ásványvíz
soft drink	üditő
ice cubes	jég kockák
coffee	kávé
tea	téa
caffeine free	koffein-mentes

INDEX

$\times$ = restaurant, ▥ = hotel

122 Index

NOTES

NOTES

NOTES

NOTES

NOTES

NOTES

NOTES

NOTES

With guidebooks for every kind of travel—from weekend
getaways to island hopping to adventures abroad—it's
easy to understand why smart travelers go with **Fodors**.

Fodor's Travel Publications

Available at bookstores everywhere. For descriptions of all our titles, a key to Fodor's guidebook series, and on-line ordering, visit www.fodors.com/books

Gold Guides

U.S.

Alaska
Arizona
Boston
California
Cape Cod,
Martha's Vineyard,
Nantucket
The Carolinas &
Georgia
Chicago
Colorado

Florida
Hawai'i
Las Vegas, Reno,
Tahoe
Los Angeles
Maine, Vermont,
New Hampshire
Maui & Lāna'i
Miami & the Keys
New England
New Orleans

New York City
Oregon
Pacific North
Coast
Philadelphia & the
Pennsylvania
Dutch Country
The Rockies
San Diego
San Francisco

Santa Fe, Taos,
Albuquerque
Seattle &
Vancouver
The South
U.S. & British
Virgin Islands
USA
Virginia &
Maryland
Washington, D.C.

Foreign

Australia
Austria
The Bahamas
Belize &
Guatemala
Bermuda
Canada
Cancún, Cozumel,
Yucatán Peninsula
Caribbean
China
Costa Rica
Cuba
The Czech
Republic &
Slovakia
Denmark

Eastern &
Central Europe
Europe
Florence, Tuscany
& Umbria
France
Germany
Great Britain
Greece
Hong Kong
India
Ireland
Israel
Italy
Japan
London

Madrid &
Barcelona
Mexico
Montréal &
Québec City
Moscow,
St. Petersburg,
Kiev
The Netherlands,
Belgium &
Luxembourg
New Zealand
Norway
Nova Scotia, New
Brunswick, Prince
Edward Island
Paris
Portugal

Provence &
the Riviera
Scandinavia
Scotland
Singapore
South Africa
South America
Southeast Asia
Spain
Sweden
Switzerland
Thailand
Toronto
Turkey
Vienna & the
Danube Valley
Vietnam

Special-Interest Guides

Adventures to
Imagine
Alaska Ports of Call
Ballpark Vacations
The Best Cruises
Caribbean Ports
of Call
The Complete
Guide to America's
National Parks
Europe Ports of Call
Family Adventures
Fodor's Gay Guide
to the USA

Fodor's How to Pack
Great American
Learning Vacations
Great American
Sports & Adventure
Vacations
Great American
Vacations
Great American
Vacations
for Travelers
with Disabilities
Halliday's
New Orleans
Food Explorer

Healthy Escapes
Kodak Guide to
Shooting Great
Travel Pictures
National Parks
and Seashores
of the East
National Parks of
the West
Nights to Imagine
Orlando Like a Pro
Rock & Roll
Traveler Great
Britain and Ireland

Rock & Roll
Traveler USA
Sunday in San
Francisco
Walt Disney
World for Adults
Weekends in
New York
Wendy Perrin's
Secrets Every
Smart Traveler
Should Know
Worlds to Imagine

Fodor's Special Series

WHEREVER YOU TRAVEL, *H*ELP IS NEVER FAR AWAY.

From planning your trip to providing travel assistance along the way, American Express® Travel Service Offices are always there to help you do more.

Budapest

American Express Military Banking
Deak Ferenc U. 10
(36) (1) 266 8680

American Express Bureau de Change
Hotel Hilton Budapest
Hess Andras Terl-3
(36) (1) 214 6446

Travel
www.americanexpress.com/travel

**American Express Travel Service Offices
are located throughout Hungary.**